SORCERERS AND ORA

Ian Mathie spent his childhood and early school years in Africa. After a short service commission in the RAF, he returned to the continent as a rural development officer working for the British government and a number of other agencies. His work in water resources and related projects during the 1970s brought him into close contact with the African people, their cultures and varied tribal customs, many of which are now all but lost. These experiences, recorded in his notebooks, were the inspiration for a series of African memoirs, of which *Sorcerers and Orange Peel* is the fifth volume. Ian continued to visit Africa until health considerations curtailed his travelling. He now lives in south Warwickshire with his wife and dog.

By the same author

SORCERERS
AND
ORANGE PEEL

To Judith,
Best wishes

Ian Mathie

Ian Mathie

MOSAÏQUEPRESS

First published in the UK in 2014 by
MOSAÏQUE PRESS
Registered office:
70 Priory Road
Kenilworth, Warwickshire CV8 1LQ
www.mosaïquepress.co.uk

Cover design by Gary Henderson
GH Graphic Design Ltd

Printed in the UK.

ISBN 978-1-906852-27-6

For Isla Grace and Phillipa Jane,
the two newest members of my tribe,

and for Helen,
who, with great dignity and courage,
has joined the ancestors.

Contents

List of illustrations and maps

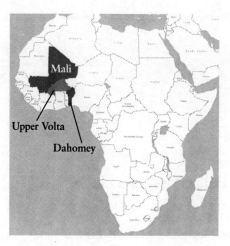

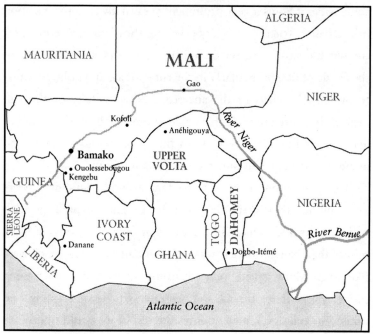

Copyright © Map Resources

Author's note

SORCERY IS A FACT OF LIFE in many African societies. Among some tribes it holds a very prominent yet usually secretive position in the tribal structure and nobody can afford to ignore or upset the witch-doctor, sorcerer or fetish priest. Superstition is part of the fabric of life, particularly in the rural areas, and nobody wants to offend the spirits or the ancestors either wilfully or through neglect. It is often the sorcerer's role to remind them of this and to act as their intermediary to keep the spirit worlds satisfied and avoid ill fortune being inflicted on the community.

Today there are a lot of charlatans around, claiming powers and abilities they certainly don't have. They exploit people's beliefs, fears and vulnerabilities for their own ends, leaving more misery than benefit in their wake. But not all sorcerers are or were like this. Many spent years learning their craft, undergoing progressively more taxing and secretive rituals of training and initiation, and developing abilities the rest of us would rightly see as magical for they often defy even the most rigorous scientific examination. Nevertheless they can do things nobody outside their guilds can explain.

It has been my privilege to live near and get to know a number of these extraordinary people since I was a child. Through participation in a number of initiation rites I have seen briefly beyond the veil, and know that they can often do what they claim. There is a whole spectrum of the world of which ordinary mortals are normally unaware. These men and women can reach into that realm and do extraordinary things.

This book is about a few of those strange beings and the impact they had on ordinary people's lives. To some it may seem fanciful – even impossible – but I assure you, having lived through it, I know it is all true.

Other books in the African Memoir Series are set in the same period and area as the events described in this book – Central Africa in the early 1970s. Many of the people and places that pass briefly through these pages appear in greater detail in the companion volumes, notably *Bride Price* and *Man in a Mud Hut*.

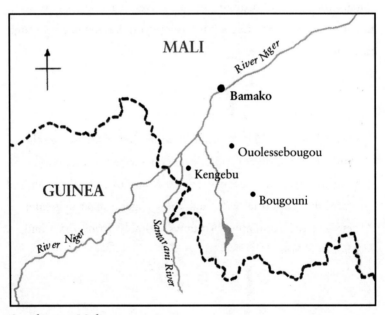

South-west Mali

PART 1

A BAD DAY
FOR DYING

The hut was a crude structure, a framework of sticks to which dried sorghum stalks had been bound with grass string to form thin rudimentary walls. The place was silent and looked deserted.

1 ~ Breakdown

IT WASN'T A ROCK that ripped the sump out of my Land Rover and brought me to a sudden, lurching halt in a gush of hot oil vapour and smoke, but it was just as hard. Oil from the engine spurted onto the hot exhaust, filling the cab with choking fumes as I slammed the gear into neutral, flung open the door and leapt from my seat. I expected the old vehicle to burst into flames at any moment. Time slipped into slow motion. The cloud of oily blue smoke took an age to disperse, drifting away on a barely discernible current of hot afternoon air. The engine began clicking as it cooled.

Standing ten yards away, gulping in clean air, I stared at the scene in despair. Across the silence of the bush the mournful call of a hoopoe echoed, offering an eerie requiem for my defunct vehicle. I looked around, trying to locate the source of its call, but the bird was as elusive as a dream. I began to wonder if, in the moments of drama, I had imagined it, until it called again.

The previous evening, while I was heading towards Sankarani, there had been no track for the last hour and I had driven through flat virgin bush. On this side of the river, the country was undulating parkland with a few flat-topped acacia trees standing about thirty feet tall. Scattered across the land were patches of short yellowing grass and numerous glossy leaved bushes that looked like laurels. The Peuhl people of the region called them *shinga'a*. There were other bushes too, with stubby hardwood skeletons and occasional clumps of thorn scrub. These scratched and screeched along the sides of the Land Rover as I passed between them. It may have been an old vehicle but it was good for the terrain, with large wheels, a powerful six-cylinder engine and four-wheel drive that would pull it out of most difficult spots. Now, however, it was stranded, the front lifting as though it was trying to rear up and do a wheelie. The scene stood frozen in time in an alien landscape, devoid of the trappings of civilisation. In fact, apart from the scrub and the trees with a few gaily coloured birds flitting between them, the land appeared empty.

Yesterday, after passing the last village near the Guinea border, my companion and I had driven for two hours and covered at least twenty-five miles before we reached the Sankarani River, a dark turbid canal fifty feet wide, flowing northeast. There we camped by the water and cooked a large fruit rat he had caught for our supper, before settling down to sleep. I awoke this morning to find my guide had gone, melting away before dawn. He had left behind a twisted twig, pointing like a finger post, to show me the direction I must take, leading me onwards into south-west Mali.

Now I was in a wilderness of empty countryside that featured as a blank space on my map. Through this land trickled myriad small watercourses and seasonal channels. These made up the headwaters of the mighty River Niger. It wasn't called that here, of course; it was known as Joliba in the Manding language spoken hereabouts. The name changes many times along the river's twenty-five hundred mile length as it flows through the territories of different racial and cultural groups, finally to emerge into the Bight of Benin through a vast delta in south-eastern Nigeria. Before that it passes through rich alluvial plains, an inland swampy delta, open desert, rolling savannah, parkland and the remains of once-dense tropical forests. Here, near the source, it was merely a series of trickles and gullies snaking their way northward out of the eastern Guinea hills.

To the south lay the thorny waste of the Guinea forest, and beyond that Sierra Leone and Liberia, the land of devils. All three countries were the homes of powerful secret sects, where heavy magic is practised, their territories still barely explored. Few outsiders went there; only a few bold missionaries had ventured in since the late nineteenth century. Those brave souls left behind little to show they had been there and the land remained largely closed to the rest of the world until extensive diamond deposits were discovered in Sierra Leone in the late 1960s.Those became the spark which triggered a vicious civil war between 1991 and 2002 with unequalled barbarism when the Liberian dictator, Charles Taylor, sought to intervene and take over the Tonga region.

The most prominent westerner to have visited was Graham Green who began in Sierra Leone and walked 450 miles through the thorny forests of Liberia in 1935, accompanied by his cousin Barbara. He wrote about it in his book *Journey Without Maps*. Even travelling on foot, he learned very little about the country or its people and virtually nothing about their secretive cultures.

To the north of me was the sparsely populated region of south-western Mali, beyond which lay the cultivated lands where the burgeoning River Niger brought life to the dark interior. It was a region unknown to the outside world until a young Scottish doctor ventured there more than a hundred and fifty years ago. His name was Mungo Park and he came to search for the River Niger. Since then, as there were no readily exploitable natural resources, nobody seemed inclined to come and do anything constructive here. Even the colonising French had largely ignored it.

AS I STOOD LOOKING at my broken vehicle, the hoopoe called again. Its haunting 'hoo-poo-poo' refrain was insistent, beckoning. I turned slowly, scanning the bushes, trying to locate the source of its call but seeing nothing. The call came again and then, as I turned my head towards where I thought it came from, I caught a brief pink flash in the edge of my vision. It was the bird taking flight, floating floppily from one bush to another.

It called again, asking me to go to it, and I took the first step towards where that fleeting image had been. Again it called and again I glimpsed it float from its perch to another bush. The first step was followed by another and then another as I followed it.

"This is ridiculous," I said aloud after walking a few yards. "I've heard all the tales about *sokago* and now here I am in thrall to it myself. It's only a bird, and I have a bust sump to mend."

I stopped and turned back.

In doing so, my eyes swept the surrounding bush and I became aware of a small hut, half hidden by bushes and a clump of elephant grass, only a few yards further on.

Had the hoopoe been leading me towards the hut? The idea seemed absurd and yet completely logical. After all, this bird is known to lead onwards those who are searching. But it doesn't normally lead them towards any worthwhile destination. That's what *sokago* is all about. It's called the wandering sickness. People who suffer from *sokago* experience an overbearing compulsion to answer the call, travelling ever on towards a destination they cannot define, yet feeling drawn forwards by the most powerful force. The hoopoe, that mysterious deceiver of the bush, is merely the hypnotic bait to entice the wanderer onward.

Well, there was no harm in having a look at the hut, I supposed. It was only a few yards further. As I walked towards it, I saw the hoopoe settle on the rough thatched roof. It cocked its crested head and looked at me as if to say, "You made the right decision." It stayed there as I approached and only when I scraped my shin on a branch sticking out from a gnarled bush was my reverie broken. I looked down to see where I was walking.

As I reached the hut, I was surprised to see the bird was still on the roof. These are normally shy, secretive birds and I was puzzled: why had it permitted me to get so close in the open like this? It wasn't normal.

It must have decided its task was fulfilled. Opening its wings, it displayed a curve of beautiful black and pink bars as it swooped from the roof and its floppy, casual flight carried it away into the scrub.

The hut was a crude structure, a framework of sticks to which dried sorghum stalks had been bound with grass string to form thin rudimentary walls. The roof had once been well thatched but now appeared badly in need of repair. The hut seemed too dilapidated to be in use but had an air about it that suggested otherwise. Although the ash was cold, a strong smell of smoke told me the fireplace outside the door had held hot coals quite recently. Even so, the place was silent and looked deserted as I made a circuit of the outside.

Coming round to the door, I heard a rustling sound from

within, followed by what sounded like a cough. As I moved toward the open doorway, I noticed a crude fetish tied to one of the uprights and paused on the threshold. Without an invitation from its owner, one does not casually enter any hut protected in this way. Nevertheless, I was curious.

The cough came again so I clapped my hands to announce my presence and leaned forward to peer inside, calling out a soft greeting. It was not as dark inside as I expected. Bright bars of sunlight streamed through the rough walls illuminating a heap of dirty rags beside an old man who sat huddled in a foetal position, his arms wrapped around his shins. His head had sunk onto his knees and his eyes were closed. Only the movement of a single finger, flicking languidly at his foot to chase away a pestering fly, showed he was alive.

Again there was a cough. It emanated from the bundle of rags. I realised there was someone else in the hut, almost completely hidden from view. As I stepped forwards to get a better look, the old man slowly raised his head and gazed at me with tired, faded eyes. He appeared unsurprised by my appearance, showed no alarm at finding a stranger entering his hut uninvited, and merely watched as I reached forward to investigate the coughing bundle of rags.

It crossed my mind that he must be one of the oldest people I had encountered in this part of West Africa, where life expectancy in the villages was seldom more than about forty years for men. This man was well into his seventies, possibly older. His skin was like dark wrinkled parchment that had been folded and unfolded many times, leaving indelible creases. Faded by the years, it was now dusty and cracked, more grey than brown, like tired milk chocolate that has been kept in the fridge improperly sealed. His hands, callused from decades of hard work, had fat knuckles where arthritis had swollen the joints; his feet were encrusted with hard cracked skin, suggesting he had never worn shoes of any sort. His hair, such as remained, was silver and wispy, its once-tight curls now looser and wrapping the back of his skull like a scruffy friar's tonsure. He wore only a faded blue shirt, several sizes too big for him, which barely concealed his emaciated frame within.

"*Lafia bela*," I said as I entered, hoping he understood my greeting. He gave a slight lift of his head, indicating his recognition of the greeting and acceptance that I meant no harm, but otherwise offered no response.

I moved forward to look more closely at the pile of rags, from which more coughing was coming. Lifting a fold of the cloth, I saw an old woman's head. Her eyes were closed and she lay on her side. When she coughed again a bubble of spittle formed on her lips, grew and then burst. The pile of rags covering her shivered slightly as her body beneath shuddered from the fit and then became still once more.

Reaching down, I felt the woman's neck for a pulse and found her skin was burning hot. Her pulse was weak and fluttering. It was obvious she had a raging fever. I wondered how long she had been like this. I turned back to the man and held his wrist. His pulse was steady and slow but his skin also felt hotter than it should have been. He too had the fever but it was not as bad as the woman's. Had it already passed the worst or was his only in the early stages?

Either way, I couldn't just walk out and leave them like this. I knew my Land Rover wasn't going anywhere until I had done some extensive repairs, and that would take time. These people needed help now and that need would not wait. I had pulled a water bottle with me from the Land Rover as I jumped clear. Now I unscrewed the cap and tipped a little water into its cup. Propping the old woman up, I held it to her lips and was pleased when she sucked the liquid into her mouth. I refilled the small cup and gave her more before turning to offer some to the old man.

As I turned from the old woman, I realised there was someone else present. It must have been a subtle shift in the light that made me look toward the doorway. What I saw made the hairs on the back of my neck stand up. I felt my skin prickle. Every nerve in my body went to red alert as I realised the figure in the doorway was a large spotted hyena. Its head was thrust forward aggressively, eyes fixed on me, its jaws open as it snarled, saliva dripping from its curled lips.

I froze.

My mind froze.

Africa is full of surprises, some of them a little frightening, but I'd never met anything like this. Of course I'd seen hyenas before, some at quite close quarters, but this was entirely different. I was trapped in this cage of rough sticks, completely unarmed, with this monster blocking the only exit. Terror does not begin to describe the emotions that coursed through me at that moment.

The hyena must have been as shocked as I was. It stared at me. I stared back. All the folklore I had ever heard said one should never look an animal like this straight in the eye. It's too much of a challenge and invites attack. But I was trapped; we'd already made eye contact and I couldn't drag my eyes away to look anywhere else.

I stared at those evil eyes and the hyena stared back, a low rumble building in its throat. Time stood still, the two of us locked in this mind-numbing stasis. The old man sat watching through rheumy eyes blurred by fever.

An eruption of coughing from the bundle of rags beside me broke the thrall and drew my eyes downwards to the old woman. I laid my hand on her shoulder, feeling the shuddering of her feeble muscles, wracked by spasms as she coughed. Slowly she became limp again as the fit passed.

Seconds later when I looked back at the doorway, afraid the hyena might be about to launch itself at me, the animal had vanished. Bright sunlight filled the space.

I was confused. Had I been imagining things?

2 ~ The dying house

IT WAS PURE CHANCE that I had entered Mali through this corner of Guinea. Normally I used a light aircraft for long-range transport but my Cessna had been grounded for a major overhaul. I had spent the last nine weeks up in the north, along the Senegal River, overseeing a series of water projects. Now I was heading home to the village where I was based in Upper Volta, but my route had been dictated by broken bridges and closed roads. As a result I had been obliged to swing further south to get into Mali and had ended up coming through the corner of Guinea.

I had long held an ambition to see the source of the River Niger. While others had long ago surveyed the great river's length and the delta had been explored, I had found almost nothing in writing about its source. This diversion gave me an ideal opportunity to visit the area and seek out the fabled Sankarani. This was supposedly one of the headwater streams that fed the River Niger. Searching for it would also enable me to explore the south-western corner of Mali, an area I had been keen to look at for a long time but had previously never had cause to visit.

Everything I had heard among the 'chatterati' back in the

capital, Bamako, suggested this was a backward region with little economic activity and no current development projects. Now I would be able to see for myself.

The people in the region were largely Mandinka subsistence farmers, growing grain as staples with a few yams and legumes in small family plots. There were also a scattering of Peuhl herdsmen, tending small herds of cattle and a few sheep and goats. The land was thinly populated, largely vacant and under-used. I wondered why this was so, in a region that should have been well watered and fertile if the huge river not far downstream was anything to go by.

A moment's inattention on my part had brought today's exploration to an unexpected halt. Now I was stranded and needing, I suspected, some major mechanical repairs to my Land Rover. To add to the delay this imposed, I had discovered two sick old people requiring immediate help.

Strangely, there appeared to be no community nearby to care for them. That alone was unusual. Africans are gregarious. The isolation of these two raised questions. The fetish on the doorpost should have alerted me to this but I was in unfamiliar territory. Each region and every individual sorcerer has his own peculiarities and distinctive features. The significance of this one had eluded me. I thought it was simply the sort of protective fetish many houses have on their door.

Since I wasn't going anywhere until the vehicle was mended, the priorities were clear. I had to do what I could to help the people in the hut until and unless some relative turned up to take over. Then I could try to repair my vehicle.

To do anything about the Land Rover, I would first have to remove it from the anthill on which it sat marooned. Either that or remove the anthill from beneath it. Since there was no way of starting the engine to drive it off the obstruction, removing the anthill was the only viable option.

The back of the vehicle was fitted with extra tanks and a series of lockers for spare parts and essential supplies. I was well equipped for emergencies like this. There was a comprehensive first aid kit with anti-malarial pills, antibiotics and other medicines. I had a plentiful supply of water in the 120-litre tank that I'd topped up that morning before leaving the Sankarani River. There was also enough dried and tinned food to keep me for several months if fresh food was unavailable. This meant there was plenty to share. It was only a question of whether it would be suitable. If all else failed, I had a catapult and a large bag of small round pebbles. My guide the previous day had had no trouble in finding something to eat when we stopped at Sankarani. The countryside hereabouts was similar enough so I could always hunt for small game if necessary, with at least some expectation of catching something.

Having sorted out the medicines I hoped might help, I decided to have a quick look around before going back to the hut and climbed onto the vehicle's cab to get a better view of the surrounding bush. This let me see well over half a mile in every direction, but there was no sign of any other habitation. I had a pair of binoculars in the cab, but even using these revealed nothing more.

One thing I did see that seemed slightly out of place, however, was a dense clump of dark green trees some way off to the south-east. They stood out against the predominant dusty grey-brown of the surrounding bush. In this late dry season, even the small glossy leaved bushes in the foreground wore a film of accumulated dust that would remain until the rains came in three months time. Everything else was parched and dry, so bright green trees looked out of place.

As I climbed down from the cab, I noticed an oddly gathered bunch of grass between me and the stick hut. Something familiar about it made me have a closer look. Many years ago it had been drummed into me that one should always pay attention to things that look out of place in the bush. This clump of grass looked out of place.

Looking at this strange twist of grass, I realised my error in ignoring the fetish sign on the door post. I should have been mentally prepared for the unexpected even if I couldn't have avoided the terrifying encounter with the spectre in the doorway. This twist of grass was definitely a warning sign that should not be ignored.

Before going back, I checked the things I had assembled and added a pair of blankets which had been sealed in plastic bags and stowed behind the seats. Since I hadn't needed them for several months, they could clearly be spared and would be much cleaner than the rags in which the old folk were presently swathed. I piled everything into an open basket, hoisted it onto my head and carried it to the shelter.

Stopping to look at the oddly shaped bunch of grass again made the hairs on the back of my neck stand up as my suspicions were confirmed. It was undoubtedly a magical symbol, put there by a sorcerer or fetish priest. Besides the bunched grass being tied with a braided raffia thread, there were three feathers, a few unusual seed pods of a species that didn't grow in this region, and a pair of long rib bones stuck in the soil so they protruded at an angle like symbolic defensive stakes.

The meaning was clear: this was protected ground. Any local person would know that and avoid the place. I had ignored the warnings and barged right in. Facing that drooling hyena as it blocked the hut's doorway began to make sense. Because it had vanished as suddenly as it appeared, I wondered at the time if it had been imaginary; whether I was seeing things that weren't there.

Now I knew that was not so. The beast had been real enough, although its coming and going were indeed magical.

Staring at that hyena's eyes, I had been aware of the muscles rippling down its flanks, as if it was preparing to launch itself at me. That moment had lasted forever, with neither of us willing to break eye contact. The old woman's coughing fit that had made me drop my gaze had been real too, and my relief at the animal's disappearance had distracted me from thinking about the wider implications and meaning of its appearance. Now I realised I should be more alert and pay attention to making sense of signs and messages that were all around me.

The realisation was almost as alarming as the hyena's unexpected appearance. It made me spin round to look in case it had appeared again. But there was nothing there. The hut was unchanged, with only the old man sitting holding his knees, the old woman coughing under her bundle of filthy rags, and me.

A faint buzzing attracted my attention. I looked up and saw a pair of hornets chewing at the bark on one of the sticks supporting the thatch. At any other time, I might have recognised these as messengers of the sorcerer, but at that moment I was only just beginning to consider such things and my mind was slow.

It may sound fanciful, in the comfort of a Western sitting room, to suggest that a sorcerer could harness insects to serve as his observers and warn of intruders, but that would be to deny the realities of life in the bush. The culture there is one in which the mundane physical world and that of the spirits are intimately entwined, constantly rubbing shoulders and each dependent on the other. Sorcerers are intermediaries between the people, who are largely unable to see beyond their own physical dimension, and the spirits. Many are also skilled herbalists; others are masters of illusion, able to perform feats that would amaze even the most adept Western conjuror. Their place in society, which is often a mystery or a reason for ridicule to most outsiders, makes perfect sense to the tribesmen they serve, and the participation of animals and insects in their affairs is accepted as normal.

Thinking about this, it was obvious that there would be similar signs around the hut, some close by, others further out. I put down my basket and went to look for them. In a few minutes, I found four more protective signs. The one thing common to all of them which struck me as odd was that none included any form of food. Nor was there any evidence that there had been any food there previously; and there was none at the hut. This confirmed that these were warning signs.

The precise nature of the warning was still obscure to me but, because of one or two elements commonly associated with traditional medicine, I took them to be a warning of disease. Then it dawned on me what this all meant: the stick hut was a dying house.

No help would be coming from whatever community these two old people belonged to. They had been isolated in the hut because of disease or simply because it was their time to die. The fever was purely a coincidental route to their death. They were not expected to survive.

At some point in the future, probably after one or two weeks, someone suitably qualified in the secret rituals would come to confirm they were dead. The stick hut, with their bodies in it, would probably be ceremonially burned and the site marked as sacred. And the members of the community would get on with their lives.

The signs told me there would be no funeral rites and no burial for these two, possibly because of the disease, but more likely because they were not normal people. There was something special separating them from the common man. Perhaps they too were sorcerers and the hyena was their totem spirit.

This left me with a dilemma and numerous questions. Would any assistance I might give offend the spirits if the old people survived as a result? Would others be upset because I had interfered in a sacred ritual? Could Western medicine cure their fever? Or were they in the process of meeting their end through a magical process outside my comprehension?

I mulled over these questions as I walked around examining the fetish signs, finally stopping where I had deposited my basket. Another fit of coughing from inside the stick hut broke into my thoughts and made the decision for me. The cough was stronger than before and suggested the old woman's condition had improved. Western medicine won the battle in my mind. I would try and help.

Would even the most rabid fetish priest condemn me for trying honestly to help ease someone's suffering, I wondered? In all likelihood, yes, he would. Then that was a risk I must take. Ignorance of their customs wouldn't even get a hearing. Secret rituals have very strict rules and woe betide those who infringe them, be they initiates or ignorant outsiders. But the penalties could be dire.

Oh well, so be it, I decided, I'll try anyway and face that if I have to.

As I picked up my basket and went into the stick hut, I thought perhaps the old couple had been left with an even chance either of dying from the fever or fighting it and recovering. In this part of the world, such an idea was not uncommon. I tried, unconvincingly, to reassure myself with the thought. Questions flooded my mind, getting in the way of constructive thinking. There was no way of knowing the answers and they mattered little; I was here now and couldn't just leave without trying to help.

The first priority was water.

Nothing had changed inside the stick hut. The woman lay wracked by fever and coughing fits. The old man sat immobile, but he watched attentively as I removed the rags from the old woman and lifted her into a semi-sitting position to give her a drink. Her frail body was little more than skin and bone and weighed next to nothing.

It was a long time since I had seen anyone so thin, not since visiting a drought relief camp in Niger, near the northern shore of Lake Chad, more than a year earlier. Then there had been thousands like this, but they were all much younger. This pair looked as if time had forgotten them, and I marvelled that they had survived so long in this harsh and unforgiving place. The open bush may hold romantic appeal for many, but it is far from being an easy place in which to live. I wondered how long these two had been here and whether this empty hut had been their lifelong home or was merely a ritual place.

The woman opened her eyes when I sat her up, staring at me with a gaze showing no sign of comprehension. Her mouth opened as I touched her lips with a plastic cup of water. After a moment, sensing the wetness on her lips, she sucked tentatively and swallowed. She must have been dry for a long time and that first swallow took an effort. As the water trickled down her parched throat her body responded; a scrawny hand came up to clasp the cup and she sucked again. After two more swallows she was taking the water almost greedily.

Before she drained the cup, I pulled it slightly away and placed two Paludrine anti-malarial tablets on her tongue, then encouraged her to drink again. She soaked up the water until it was all gone and the pills with it. That had been easier than I expected.

Peeling the stinking rags off, I wrapped one of my blankets round her and made sure she was firmly propped against the supporting poles of the hut. After this, I turned my attention to the old man. As I if refilled the water cup and held it out to him, his eyes took on a new look, like hope reborn. He released his grip on the bony knee and wrapped his gnarled fingers round the red mug. His eyes flicked from me to the water in the cup and back to me as he lifted it to his lips and drank the whole lot in one amazingly slow draft. It was as though he hadn't had a drink for a month and was determined to savour every drop.

There was an old foam rubber mattress in my Land Rover which I normally used as padding to stop things rattling about in the back, since its usefulness as a sleeping pad was long past. It might be old, but it would give the woman more comfort than leaning against the knobbly bark of the hut's poles with only a blanket for padding. I went and pulled it out while considering what to do next.

It was obvious I couldn't go anywhere until the damaged sump was repaired, and I didn't yet know how extensive the damage was. There was no certainty I would be able to mend it on my own and it might be necessary to walk out from here and get help. Without a clear idea of where 'here' was, that would be a challenge. I knew I was close to the Guinea border, somewhere between Kanbaya and Badalé, but it was impossible to be certain. Neither of these places was actually marked on the map. I had only the somewhat theatrical gesticulations and telegraphic pointing of my former guide, together with his incessant repetition of these names, on which to base my assumptions. So it seemed sensible to reconcile myself to being here for a few days while I tried to mend the Land Rover. This would give me plenty of time to care for these two old people until their fever had subsided. After that I could decide what to do for their future well-being and support.

As I pulled the rubber pad from where it was wedged, a cardboard box it had been supporting finally collapsed, spilling food tins onto the floor of the truck. I selected a small can of corned beef and another of vegetable soup and took these with me to the stick hut, along with a can opener and a spoon. If the old folk could swallow water, they might be able to swallow soup. A little corned beef mashed into the soup would add nourishment without being too rich. It was likely they hadn't eaten for days so it was important not to give them too much to start with.

I WAS ALONE IN THE vastness of West Africa with a broken vehicle and no means of letting anyone know where I was. Normally someone had a copy of my itinerary, with approximate dates and contact points. This was long before the days of mobile phones so there was no way of telling anyone of my situation and beyond telling the manager of the well school the date when I expected to be back in Bamako and giving him a very sketchy outline of my intended route, I had told nobody of my travel plans. This was a scouting mission and I really was on my own. With the unusual situation I had encountered and the likely complications of sorcery now apparent, it was going to be an interesting interlude.

Surprisingly, it didn't at this point feel threatening. Or maybe I was being too stupid to recognise the dangers.

3 ~ Round 1 to the anthill

I SPENT THE AFTERNOON making a thin soup with mashed corned beef in it and feeding this in small quantities to the old people in the stick hut. It required little effort to get a small fire going in the hearth outside the hut's door and it took only a few moments to scour out the small earthenware cooking pot that lay beside the fireplace. Later I would use this same cooking pot and fire to make some millet porridge, but soup was quicker to make and I wanted to get some food into them as soon as possible.

Feeding the old woman was not easy. With one hand holding her up, it was difficult to spoon soup into her slack mouth without spilling it all over her. Eventually I put some in the red plastic mug and held this to her lips. This seemed to work better and in about ten minutes she took a little over half of it.

The old man was able to hold the mug himself. He sipped the soup slowly; savouring every mouthful as his eyes gradually lost their faded hopelessness and took on a new interest. He still sat hunched, clutching his knees with one arm. I wondered how long he had been sitting like that and whether he would be able to move. Depending on how his digestive system responded to the soup, that might become necessary in a hurry. It wasn't unusual for people who had been starved to have a severe reaction to food and for it to go straight through. Oh well, I thought, we'll tackle that if it happens.

Once I was satisfied that both had swallowed some soup and anti-malarial pills and I'd given them more water, I went back to look at the Land Rover and consider what to do about it. It was clear that I couldn't drive it backwards off the anthill. In any case, it was doubtful if the engine would start and I didn't want to risk doing more damage. The only alternative was to get underneath and dig the anthill away. That was not going to be easy.

What I really needed, I thought, was a tame aardvark to rip it apart with his claws. There was little chance of that as aardvarks are shy, generally nocturnal beasts. I have heard it said that the camel is a horse designed by a committee. If that's so, the aardvark must surely have been the committee's second attempt. It looks like a childish hybrid between a donkey, a pig and a kangaroo, armed with the claws of a velociraptor.

Ungainly though they may appear, aardvarks are prodigious diggers and can excavate a four-foot deep hole to conceal themselves in less than five minutes. They can do this in the hardest of ground and, judging by the number of their holes I had passed in the two hours before I hit the anthill, they were common in this region. So, of course, were the termites on which they feed as there were termite castles everywhere.

Across all the lateritic regions of West Africa, termites build statuesque castles that stand like stalagmites of red earth, baked by the scorching sun to the hardness of rock. In many places, these are solitary structures as tall as fifteen feet, appearing for all the world like they were made for a Disney cartoon. In other places,

Termite mounds... warty encrustations on the rocky landscape.
Photo: Trevor Kittelty

they are smaller but clustered together in great colonies like a stockpile of dragon's teeth.

Here, they looked like warty encrustations on the landscape, more akin to stromatolites than the elegant structures I was familiar with. The landscape had been changing as I drove further from the Sankarani River, but it was the change in the style of the termite mounds that particularly stood out. I had stopped and broken off an overhanging piece to see what it was. It was only then, finding the inside teeming with termites, that I understood. They might have been a different species of termite or it might have been the soil that obliged them to build in this way, but the contrast was remarkable.

WITH SMALL FLUFFY CLOUDS passing slowly overhead, the air was warm but calm. It was as if the countryside was holding its breath, waiting for me to do something. Nature seemed to have conspired to make me pause, for I could now see it was one of the mushroom anthills that had brought me to an unintended halt, and there were acres of them through which I would have to navigate to get away from here.

Was this another strange sign telling me I must stay awhile? After the hoopoe that led me to discover the stick hut, the fetish signs ringing the place and on the doorway, and that awful apparition, I wondered. Whatever it was, my next priority had to be to get access to the crushed sump and assess the damage. That meant shifting the anthill.

The impact had lifted the front wheels; they were no longer touching the ground. The mass of the anthill was wedged solidly under the vehicle. Even if it would start and I tried to reverse, it was unlikely I'd be able to drive it off before the engine seized. From front to back, it was jammed on top of the anthill. Apart from the oil that had soaked into the top of the mound, there was little I could see to tell me how bad the damage was. The anthill looked relatively intact. I would somehow have to move the vehicle off it or dig the anthill away to get a proper look at the sump.

The winch on the front was no help as it required engine power to drive it. The only tools I had that might be of any use at this stage were a pair of tyre levers, a machete and a traditional hoe. I had a shovel too, but the handle was broken and needed replacement before I could use it.

There was no alternative: digging away the anthill a little at a time and clearing a space to make repairs was the only option. It was going to be a slow task. I wondered briefly about hand-cranking the winch to pull the vehicle forwards over the anthill, but the cable was not very long and the nearest suitable tree to anchor it to was more than a hundred yards away, and not directly in front. In any case, dragging the vehicle forward was a stupid idea; the differential on the back axle would certainly get caught on the same obstruction.

Lying on my side between the front wheels, hacking at the anthill with my hoe was both uncomfortable and tiring work. It was hot and smelly in the confined space. Occasional drips of black oil falling into my ear irritated and caused me to bang my head. It was not the kind of job designed to put me in the sweetest of tempers and the realisation that it could have been avoided if my concentration had been sharper compounded the mood.

Nine pints of oil soaking into the anthill had done little to soften the structure and make it easier to demolish, so every small flake I managed to chip off seemed like a victory. It made me marvel at the engineering skills of the insignificant insects that had built this anthill, and envious of the capacity of their ungainly predators to rip the structures open with apparent ease.

If only one would come along now and help me.

But no, the smell of scorched motor oil and my presence would put it off; I was on my own here.

After an hour, I had chipped off less than fifteen pounds of rock-like earth and my vehicle hadn't budged. The sun was now directly overhead and my knees and lower legs were being scorched while the rest of me sweltered in the cramped space beneath the engine. I slid out and climbed to my feet.

REMEMBERING THE OLD PEOPLE in the stick hut, I wandered over to see how they were getting on. Both appeared to be exactly as I had left them. I had placed the water bottle and cup beside the old man in the hope that he would use it and maybe give some to the woman, but the cup still sat with the water in it, a light film of dust now coating its surface. A line of small ants led up and over the rim and they were dipping in to refresh themselves.

I swilled out the cup, refilled it and gave the woman another drink, making sure that she took a whole cupful. She looked so dehydrated that she probably needed fluid intravenously. It was a slow process with just a cup but gradually she absorbed the water I offered.

The old man watched me with his faded eyes, accepting the cup and drinking when I passed it to him. His eyes followed my movements as I gathered up the stinking rags the woman had been wrapped in, pushed them outside and then used a bunch of leaves from a nearby bush to sweep out the floor of the hut.

The woman was still feverish, coughing occasionally, and her skin felt cold and clammy. I wrapped her well in the blanket and laid her down on the old rubber mattress, propping up the bit under her head to lift it a little. The old man watched, unmoving, until I indicated he should drink more. He slowly picked up the cup and sipped at the water, seeming reluctant to drink it all until I shook the bottle to show him there was plenty more. Then he raised the cup, looked at it for a moment in thanks for a divine blessing and drained it. I refilled the cup and indicated he should drink again but a slight shake of the head said he would take no more.

Their dehydration made me think it would be a good idea to put some salts into the next ration of soup I gave them. There was still more soup in the pot, which I had covered with a sheet of foil to keep ants out and left warming over the embers of the fire. I too would need food soon, so I went back to the Land Rover to get the salt, flour and an iron sheet that would enable me to make flat bread.

Back at my immobilised vehicle, I decided to have another look at the surrounding countryside. From the roof of the cab, I used my binoculars to study the dark green trees I had noticed before. Distances can be deceptive, especially in the shimmering heat haze of the open bush, but they appeared to be the best part of a mile away. I decided they could be explored later. In the opposite direction, about three hundred yards beyond the hut, there was a gully. I wondered if it held any water. The rainy season was not far off and there had already been a few showers in the area. The headwaters of the River Niger came from this area and some of the gullies carried a permanent stream. Perhaps this would turn out to be one of the feeder streams. Maybe this was what Mungo Park had missed a hundred or so years ago, I thought. But he had travelled two hundred and fifty miles north of this region and there were so many channels it would have been impossible for him to have identified one as the core of the great river. The streams only coalesced some way downstream from here.

I could see nothing else of particular interest and so climbed down and collected the supplies I had come for.

IN THE SHORT WALK between the Land Rover and the gully, I saw four snakes, which surprised me. While snakes are not uncommon, it is unusual to see so many in the open in such a small area. As I walked along the gully I saw two more nondescript brown forms slithering quietly out of view behind clumps of vegetation or into the shadow beneath thick bushes. It was a good thing there were few people in this area. Such perfectly normal behaviour on the part of the snakes would have resulted in most tribesmen pelting the bush with stones or hacking at it with long sticks in an attempt to kill the snake. Worse still, they might have set fire to the grass, hoping to exterminate them that way. While this action could result in the demise of the snake, it was equally likely to result in someone getting bitten or badly burned. Such actions soon became the self-perpetuating source for a generalised fear of snakes.

I had not seen them clearly enough to identify what species the snakes were and had no wish to step on a horned viper, so made a mental note to watch where I was putting my feet. I decided also to wear my sunglasses when walking around in this bush, as at least one of the serpents I had seen had been long and black. It could well have been a spitting cobra, whose spittle can blind a man for days while its nasty venomous bite – which often follows its spit – can kill.

My knowledge of spitting cobras was first-hand, having been bitten by one as a teenager. Fortunately, on that occasion, I had been wearing dark glasses and got none of the spittle in my eyes, but I could testify to the accuracy of the cobra's aim from more than ten feet away. I could also vouch for the power of its bite. The radical first aid for that was to cut my own leg upstream of the bite and make it bleed profusely to clear as much venom from my system as possible. I then walked four miles to the nearest medical post to get help. Fortunately they had had a supply of antivenin and my outcome had been only a few days of discomfort, but I knew of men who had died from similar bites. I now carried five vials of antivenin in the first aid kit which lived under my driving seat.

The first four hundred yards of the gully turned out to be dry so I turned back to the hut. The old woman was sleeping and seemed a little more relaxed than the last time I had looked at her. The old man still sat holding his knees. He opened his eyes as I entered, his initial look of confusion dissolving rapidly into recognition. He looked down at the plastic cup and I saw that he had drunk it dry so I refilled it, receiving a slight lift of his head in thanks as he picked it up and drank again.

Time had crept by without my noticing it. A shift in the bright bars of sunlight coming through the corn stalk wall of the hut reminded me the day was advancing. It was time to give these two some more soup, but this time I wanted to thicken it a little. I added some millet flour to give it substance, and stoked up the embers to let this cook through. I also added salt in the hope it might make up for some of the salts they must have lost. It would make recovery from the dehydration easier and might ease the cramps which would almost certainly attack their muscles when either of them tried to move.

Ten minutes later, I tipped some thickened soup into the red mug and offered it to the old man. He looked at it, sniffed it and then placed it on the ground beside him. I wondered what was wrong with it and made more drinking gestures. He just stared at me. I had put some into another mug to give to the woman and used a spoon to show him that he should eat. As I put the spoon to my mouth I realised what the problem was: the soup was too hot. I put the bowl down and waited a few minutes until it cooled. This time, when I offered the cup to the old man, he drank and his eyes lit up, twinkling in the slanting sunlight as the taste awakened his senses. I wondered again how long it had been since he had last had food and turned my attention to the old woman. She was asleep.

It seemed a shame to wake her now that she was sleeping, but she needed nourishment to fight the infection. This was more important than sleep. If she had the sustenance, she could sleep in comfort. It was not hard to prop her up and holding a spoon of warm soup to her lips produced a reflex swallow as I tipped it into her opening mouth. Slowly, so slowly, I tipped small spoonfuls in and she swallowed, her eyes still closed and her body relaxed. When she had taken half a cupful, I gave her more water and laid her down to sleep again.

The old man had finished his soup so I rinsed the cup and refilled it with water. Hungry by now, I took a bowl of soup for myself and sat where the old man could see me as I ate it.

The sun was heading towards the horizon but there was time for a bit more hacking at the anthill before darkness descended. The task would require a lot of work before I could begin to think about repairing the sump.

Leaving the old people to rest, I returned to my labours, taking a good drink of water myself before I climbed under the front bumper. I attacked from a different angle and must have found a weaker part of the structure as several large lumps came off quite easily. It was encouraging but progress was still painfully slow. Clearly the job was not going to be completed before nightfall. In fact it was slow enough to need days of work before I could begin to do anything mechanical on the engine.

4 ~ Night chorus

DARKNESS COMES QUICKLY in the African bush. As the sun reached the horizon, it was too dim to see what I was doing under the Land Rover. By the time I had climbed to my feet and brushed off the dust and debris from the anthill, the darkness was almost complete. It really happens that fast.

Stars blazed overhead in a clear sky. A thin waning moon was just rising but it gave little light so I opened a locker, brought out a well-used hurricane lamp and lit it. The yellow flame cast a soft glow a few feet in front of me as I walked across to the stick hut to check on the old people again. The old man was asleep when I arrived and it was clear the woman hadn't moved. There was still some soup in the pot. I blew life into the dying fire, added a few more twigs and set it to warm again. The sounds woke the old man. He raised his head to watch me with tired eyes. Making sure that the lamp shed enough light on my face so he could see clearly and know what I was doing, I took another close look at the old woman. Her fever had abated slightly and she was calm, her skin less clammy than before. Her pulse was steadier too. I wondered if she was past the worst or if this was just a lull.

When the soup had warmed but was not too hot, I filled the mug and offered it to the old man. His scrawny fingers clasped it firmly and he raised it immediately to his mouth. I left the old woman sleeping this time. She could have more soup and water when she woke.

Outside, the nightly chorus of insects was livening up and offered a busy backdrop of sound as I hung the lamp from a rickety rafter and looked around the stick hut with more attention. Apart from one old and well-used food pot and the two old people, I could see no possessions of any kind. Surely if this was their home they would have had something, I thought. I considered again the idea that this was a dying house, hastily erected for the purpose. But it didn't seem to be a new structure; the roof had clearly been properly made, although the thatch was now a little thin in places. I looked more carefully to see if it bore any symbols that might have signified its purpose, thinking someone might have left signs or gifts for the spirits. But I could see none, or none that I recognised.

I examined the old man carefully to see if the amulets he wore included any new ones that might have been prepared to send him on his final journey with protection. Those round his upper arm and neck were all old and had obviously been worn for a long time. Even so, he had more than a few of them and this set me to wondering. Why would a man wear so many amulets? Either he needed protection against a lot of different things or this man was more than he appeared. This made him interesting. He hadn't yet spoken and I wondered if we shared any common language. If we did, there was much I could learn from him when he recovered enough, always assuming he was willing to tell me.

I HAVE NO IDEA HOW long I sat dreaming. A sharp bark outside brought my attention back to the here and now. The hurricane lamp was beginning to flicker and when I shook it I realised it needed refilling and its wick needed cleaning. Even so, it still gave enough light to see the others in the hut. The old woman was sleeping soundly. The old man sat in the same position but his condition seemed to have deteriorated. The skin on his forehead was beaded with sweat. I reached over and touched his arm and found his skin was hot. The fever was rising and it wouldn't be long before he was shivering and shuddering. I pulled the other blanket from its plastic wrapping and draped it round him.

The jackal barked again, still some way off, but further round this time, as if it was circling at a safe distance. I wondered if it would dare come closer and got up to add more fuel to the fire and blow it back into flaming life. Once it was burning well, I added a few green leaves to make smoke in the hope that this would deter the jackal or anything else that was out there from approaching too close. The smell of fire was a deterrent to many things, not the least among them scavengers like the jackal. I had enough to deal with without having to fend off hungry scavengers and predators. A bit of smoke might help to ward off night flying insects too, especially if a little of it drifted inside the hut.

Once the fire was burning strongly, I took a few coals and started a second one a few yards away, round by the side of the hut. It only took a few moments to rip up some dry grass, collect a few sticks and make a merry blaze. When this was burning well, I took the hurricane lamp and went to the Land Rover for more paraffin. From the driver's door pocket, I also collected my catapult and a bag of pebbles. These might be useful for fending off intruders if any came too close or, in the early morning, for hunting some fresh meat in the surrounding bush.

It was past midnight, the moon was more than half way across the sky and the temperature had fallen. It wasn't cold, but the difference from mid afternoon was noticeable. I pulled out a sweater, put it on and stood listening to the night for a few minutes. From time to time I heard the characteristic 'churr' of a nightjar, interspersed with the more strident calls that I thought might be some variety of owl. There were also rustlings as small creatures moved about in the grass and I realised that these would probably be small rodents. Snakes, being cold blooded, would mostly be inactive until the sun warmed them in the morning, so the small mammals had a few hours of comparative safety in which to forage and go about their business. There was also the musical hum and buzz from countless insects. They sat scraping away at their saw-edged legs, creating the background chorus to all the other nocturnal sounds.

To anyone of a nervous disposition, this would have been purgatory, alone in the middle of nowhere. But I found it reassuring to know there was so much life all around. I had the distinct impression that the two old people in the stick hut were on the brink and was worried that one or other might not last the night. Being surrounded by such vibrant life was reassuring as it made this sad outcome feel less likely. It gave me hope for them.

Shielding my eyes against the glare from the refilled lamp, I looked around the bush as I walked back. I caught no glint of reflection from watching eyes. The faint rustling sounds in the grass and among the bushes continued, but there was no sign of patrolling scavengers. I hoped the smoke from my fires had persuaded the jackal, and any friends he might have had following him, to move on. Some of the smoke from the fire outside the doorway had drifted in between the canes of the wall. A thin blue haze now hung three feet above the floor. I was grateful for this. It meant that there were neither flies nor mosquitoes around us.

The two occupants were as I had left them and everything else seemed the same.

I poured more water into the cup and lifted the old woman to a sitting position. She stirred slightly but didn't wake properly even when I put the cup to her cracked lips. The reflex was still there and after she had swallowed a cupful I laid her down again to rest. The old man was unresponsive, even when I shook his arm gently. In the dim light, I couldn't decide whether he was heavily asleep or unable to respond because the fever gripped him. I hoped it was the former and the soup and water I had got him to swallow earlier would give him the strength to get through the night.

Arranging a few sticks across the doorway so that anything or anyone who tried to enter would make a noise, I settled down to catch some sleep while I had the chance. Besides trying to fix my broken vehicle, I knew my time could be fully occupied looking after these two when daylight came.

DIM GREY LIGHT WAS spilling in through the open doorway when I woke. It was almost dawn. The nocturnal buzz of insects and rustling of small mammals in the surrounding grass had ceased. The world was still, holding its breath, waiting for sunrise and the birth of a new day. Would this be the last day for one or both of the two who shared this ragged hut with me? It was an unwelcome idea so early in the morning as I roused myself to check on them.

The old man was still exactly as he had been the last time I looked at him in the early hours, but sweat no longer beaded his brow. The old woman was feverish again and coughing. I listened to the tone of her coughing and decided it was stronger, less ragged than it had been the previous day. I hoped I wasn't deluding myself, taking this as a sign of improvement. I propped her up, fed her more anti-malarial pills and another cup of water. She accepted them without opening her eyes, but without resistance too, so I decided the signs were positive.

A few minutes later, when I looked again, she was shivering and her skin was hot as the fever took her once more. This was the opposite of improvement. I began to bathe her forehead with water. A little dribbled down her cheek to the corner of her mouth and she sucked at it so I offered her the cup again and she swallowed some more.

Daylight arrives as rapidly as darkness. The doorway of the stick hut faced east; the inside was flooded with golden light as soon as the sun broke free of the distant horizon. Everything started to warm up rapidly as the sun climbed into the empty blue sky.

Soon after dawn the old man woke. The sparkle of his watching eyes caught my attention. I checked to see that he still had water, felt his forehead, decided he didn't have a temperature and then returned to bathing the old woman's face and neck as she was now sweating profusely and shuddering with the ravages of fever.

Half an hour later, when she was calm again, I went outside to resurrect the cooking fire. I was aware of a rank smell, something between dried blood and rotting flesh. I also had the distinctly creepy feeling of someone, or something, watching me. The stench reminded me of carrion, but it could equally have been a foul smelling fungus that had produced a fruiting body during the night and released its malodorous spores into the dawn. I looked around carefully but saw nothing.

It was only when I stood up from the fire and turned to go back into the hut that I saw him, standing a few yards away. At first I wasn't sure he was real, but a slight movement of his upper lip told me he was. Surrounded by a shimmering cloud of small flies, he was undoubtedly the source of the evil smell, although he seemed indifferent to both. He just stood, unmoving, staring at me with bloodshot eyes, his gaze boring into me like an inquisitorial gimlet.

Time stood still. For what was probably only a few seconds, but felt like an hour, I remained staring at him, transfixed. His eyes held mine and his mouth began to dribble, a long tail of saliva drooling from his jaw. It was undoubtedly the same hyena that had filled the doorway the previous day; a broad, distinctive scar ran down the right side of his face.

His stance was hostile, pent up as before, ready to hurl himself at me. The air between us almost crackled with the tension. The beast had but a few yards of sparse grass to cover and I had nothing to hand with which to defend myself if he chose to attack. My numb mind refused to formulate any plan. We stood and stared.

Suddenly the haunting, doleful call of the hoopoe echoed across the bush. I caught the pink flash of its wings in the edge of my vision as it flopped from one bush to another. I wanted to turn and look but my eyes were held fast by the hateful creature so few yards away.

The hoopoe hooted again. This time I did look, just for a fleeting second.

When I looked back, the hyena was gone. In its place stood a man, clothed in tufts of raffia and animal skins, among which the blotchy pelt of a hyena was prominent. His cheeks were scarred with marks like whiskers and he carried a broad, unforgettable scar down the side of his face. His skin was blotchy like a spotted hyena, and he wore a cluster of brightly coloured beads in his left ear lobe. One arm was wound round in a spiral with what looked like a snake, his hand protruding as if from the snake's mouth. The other hand carried a horse-tail fly whisk with which he flapped away the cluster of small flies that still buzzed around him.

Had I been seeing things, or had there been a hyena standing tin that spot only moments before? Thoughts raced, trying to sort out the anomalies of this situation and finding no clear answers.

Out of nowhere, lines of Shakespeare came into my head: *All the world's a stage and men and women merely players: they have their exits and their entrances, and one man in his time plays many parts.* What part was this man playing? Was he healer, guardian, or the man with the scythe? Was death the short-term prospect for these two old people? And why those lines? Something had made me think of them at that precise moment.

This place was rapidly producing more questions than answers, and that was unsettling.

There was another tense pause that lasted for eternity before the man spoke, delivering words I didn't understand as he gestured towards the stick hut with his fly whisk. From the tone and his posture, it was easy enough to guess he was asking about the two old people inside so I nodded and gestured with my hands to indicate that they were still alive and being cared for.

He continued to stare at me and after a moment, walked forward, still holding my gaze until he came within a yard of me. At the last moment he turned aside and went into the hut.

Without hesitating, I followed him in, seeing him crouch and reach out to touch the old woman's brow. Holding his hand against her head for almost half a minute, remaining motionless the while, he said nothing. After a while he turned to look at the old man.

Still sitting as he had been since my arrival the day before, the old man was awake now and gazed at the sorcerer – for there was no doubt that is what he was – with his washed-out grey eyes. The strange man reached out and put his hand on the old man's forehead as he had the old woman's, sitting back on his heels as he did so.

During the long moment of silence that followed, it felt as if I was on trial. Here was the judge examining the evidence. In a moment he would give his verdict, then either pass sentence for interfering in something sacred, or acquit me for trying to help these old, sick people.

I lowered myself slowly to squat at the same level as everyone else. Minutes crawled past.

That he was a sorcerer was beyond question, and he was probably a traditional medicine man as well. But whether he would accept my presence or resent my interference was far from clear. For the moment, he ignored me completely, his attention fixed on the old man. He mumbled something which, again, I didn't understand. Picking up the plastic cup I had given the old man to drink from, he sniffed the contents. He mumbled something else and the old man's eyes flicked briefly in my direction, a slight movement of his head giving confirmation that I had provided the cup and the water.

The sorcerer dipped a finger in the water and tasted it, then put the cup back on the ground beside the old man. He looked around the inside of the stick hut and saw the small bowl from which I had fed the old woman soup. Picking this up and sniffing it, he mumbled again as if repeating his former question.

Again the old man's eyes flicked in my direction and he repeated the gesture when the sorcerer touched the blanket draped around him and enquired about this. There was another long silence before the sorcerer turned and looked directly at me.

"*Hakim. Buru gai a emoa'amulla*," he said.

I had no idea what this meant so I just smiled and nodded, trying to remain calm, trying to look neither guilty nor hostile. To my greeting in Bambara, he just stared at me. I tried the greeting in Moré and then French, with the same result but it brought a flicker of recognition to his pale eyes. They were sandy coloured, almost golden like an animal's. I remembered the fearsome gaze of the hyena that was glaring at me outside such a short time ago.

Assuming from this minimal response that he understood some French, or at least recognised the language, I told him that I had found these two old people sick with fever the previous day. I told him I had given them medicine for their fever, food and water. The fever was a little less today. My vehicle was broken, so I would stay and try to help for a few days while I mended it.

The sorcerer stared at me thoughtfully for almost a minute. His gaze intense and unwavering, as if looking deep into my soul. Eventually he turned to the old man and said something in their tongue.

The old man nodded, picked up the plastic cup and drained it, then offered it to the sorcerer. He held it out to me. I refilled it from the water bottle and handed it back. With a slight nod he accepted the cup, drank most of the contents slowly and then placed it on the ground by the old man's hand. With fluid grace, he rose smoothly to his feet, nodded firmly to me and walked out into the early morning sunshine.

I wasn't sure what to think as I followed him out. He was looking at the cooking pot I had used the previous day. I told him I had made soup. I would give them more today. He must have understood for he nodded again, looking me straight in the eye as he did so. Then, without a word, he turned and walked away into the bush.

Had I done the right thing? Was his departure in this way confirmation of it?

The whole experience had been surreal, as if it had all been a dream. But it had been real enough. The scuff in the dust made by his foot as he turned to walk away was real, and with his departure the rank smell of hyena had gone as well.

After several minutes, I went back into the hut to check on my patients. The woman was still in the grip of fever, but it seemed less severe. I sat her up, administered more pills and another cup of water. The old man was more alert than he had been the previous day so I gave him pills and water too and told him I would make more soup soon. It concerned me that he was still sitting hunched as I had found him. His muscles would surely protest when he tried to move. I tried to suggest he should lie down, but he shook his head firmly and remained as he was.

THERE WAS NOTHING MORE I could do for a couple of hours so I returned to the vehicle to continue trying to demolish the anthill. As I passed the spot where the hyena had stood, I stopped to look at the ground. Two clear pug marks in the dust confirmed that the animal had been there. How, then, had it vanished so suddenly to be replaced by the man? It happened in that split second that my gaze was averted. I had no answer to this. Some things a sorcerer can do aren't readily explained, even to an open mind that has seen such power before. Even to initiates, not all would be clearly visible, and I was no initiate of this man's cult.

5 ~ A victory of sorts

THE AIR WAS STILL COOL as I rolled under the front of the stranded vehicle to resume hacking at the anthill. This morning the blade of my hoe bit more readily into the rock-hard structure. Soon fist-sized lumps were breaking loose. After an hour, I had to stop digging and clear the debris as it was beginning to get in the way. It was also seething with termites for I had finally broken into an inhabited part of the castle. The anthill now emitted a bitter ammoniac smell, like stale urine. The termites were generating pheromones to warn their clones that the colony was under attack.

After the musty aromas of the stick hut, the rank smell of the hyena, and the pungent pong that hung around the sorcerer, it seemed this place held quite a catalogue of foul odours.

In need of fresh air, I rolled out and stood up to ease my cramped muscles by walking around a little. This brought me close to one of the twisted grass signs I had inspected the day before and I noticed that it looked different. Some of the seedpods had disappeared and a bunch of fresh leaves now sprouted from the middle of the grass bundle.

This made me curious so I walked around to look at the other signs that ringed the stick hut. Every one of them had been altered. What had most definitely been warning signs before now had an aspect of hope about them in the fresh leaves. Some even had fresh grass added. Was this a sign that the sorcerer accepted or even approved of my presence and what I had done? There was no way of asking, yet I felt reassured. Any anxiety I felt before slipped away and my confidence felt renewed.

The sorcerer must have put these leaves here, yet I'd been unaware of his proximity after he walked off. The smell emanating from his skins and clothing could hardly be missed and should surely have warned me he was close. But I'd noticed nothing. It must have taken some time for him to make the changes to his signs and it was only in the last few moments before I stopped digging that the termites had begun their stink. The smell from the broken anthill was too recent to have hidden his presence. It was another demonstration of his extraordinary abilities, as if he was giving me lessons in easy stages to ensure his power would be understood and respected. I wondered what price he was going to exact for my involvement in something that hadn't been my business. There is always a quid pro quo.

AFTER ANOTHER HOUR of digging, I returned to the hut and prepared another pot of soup. The old woman had passed the fever crisis and now lay sleeping soundly, her pulse steady and her temperature dropping at last. I sat her up and fed her more pills and water while the soup simmered over low coals. Then I turned my attention to the old man.

Rather than trying to move him, I sat down opposite him in the same way he was seated and stretched out both arms to the side. He watched me closely and when I pointed to him and repeated the gesture, he slowly tried to copy me. I could see it wasn't easy, but he tried and I smiled. I moved my legs, one at a time, until they were straight out in front of me. He moved one leg, but winced as he extended it so I shook my head and said "Stop." He stopped and pulled his leg back.

I pointed to the other leg and after a moment he moved that until it hurt too much and he pulled that back as well. This was going to take time. I refilled the water cup and left him to sit and rest while I had a look at the soup. When it was ready, I put some into the plastic mug and gave it to him, then brought more for the old woman in a bowl. She woke when I lifted her to a sitting position and stared at me with some confusion, but she accepted the soup when I began spooning it into her mouth and pursed her lips, turning away slightly when she would take no more. I offered her some water and she drank half a cup. This was progress.

I sat and ate a little soup myself as the two old folk watched. Then I tidied up and went back to my digging. Leaving them both sitting with a full cup of water, the old woman propped against the corner of the hut as she had been before.

BENEATH THE LAND Rover, with the debris from my earlier efforts cleared away, I could see more of the bottom of my engine. The right side of the sump appeared intact, although it had been crushed upwards. The left side was a mess and with my finger I detected a sharp edge covered by oily grime. This was probably a split in the casing and I feared the worst. It looked as if I was going to need a workshop to mend it. More would be revealed as I removed the anthill.

The seething mass of termites exposed by my earlier

excavations had somehow vanished. I wasn't sure if something had come along during my absence at the stick hut and hoovered them up, or whether they had all retreated deeper inside their ruined castle. Either way, there was barely an insect to be seen as I resumed digging.

The inner structures of the anthill were not as hard as the outside. I was making sufficient progress to be hopeful of exposing the whole sump before the end of the day. Whether this would give me enough room to remove the damaged part was still uncertain, but it made me attack with renewed gusto. Flake by flake, the thing gradually diminished until it occurred to me there was barely enough left to continue supporting the weight of the Land Rover.

I climbed out and went for another walk to look for rocks.

There were so many other things to look at in the surrounding bush: a hornet's nest in a small tree, a cluster of pendulous weaver birds' nests in another tree, other anthills, birds, jumping crickets and another snake. Distracted by all these, it took me an hour to find two rocks large enough to put under the chassis to stop the thing collapsing on me when I dug away the remainder of the anthill. By the time I'd done this, it was early afternoon and I had left the two old people alone for several hours.

After checking them briefly and administering more pills and water, I returned to my digging, determined to get enough of the anthill removed to create a clear gap between it and the bottom of the engine before darkness overtook me.

With the chassis now propped on two rocks, it occurred to me that I might improve access by removing the wheels. It did make getting at the anthill from the side considerably easier, particularly towards the back of the engine. But the work had gone slower than I'd hoped. The sun was approaching the horizon, diminishing the light underneath the vehicle. My shoulders and hips were battered and bruised from lying on the stony ground and moving about trying to swing the hoe. My knuckles were raw from bashing them on the chassis and I realised I had drunk very little despite the heat.

With a last swing of the hoe, a chunk fell off which finally revealed a clear gap between the anthill and the engine and I cheered my success. It was time to stop, take a long drink and start thinking about food for everyone. I wondered if the sorcerer had been back to look at the old folk in my absence.

When I stood up and tried to brush off the accumulated dirt, I realised how much my body ached. I might have won this battle with the anthill, but it had exacted quite a price. You had to respect those little white insects and their marvellous engineering. I felt a moment of sadness at having to destroy all their work but then reasoned that if it hadn't been me, it could well have been a hungry aardvark that came and wrecked their home. It would have eaten most of the inhabitants as well. I had at least left them free to retreat to a secure underground chamber. Life is tough and there can be no place for Western sentimentality in the African bush.

I went to prepare food.

6 ~ Recovery and collapse

I SCOUTED AROUND AND found enough firewood to get the cooking fire going again and set a pot of water to boil. There were packets of dried vegetables among the stores in the back of my Land Rover, so I fetched some of these and another small tin of corned beef to make a tasty soup that I could thicken with millet flour. I hoped this would be sufficiently nourishing without being a problem for the starved bodies of the old folk. So far we'd been lucky; there'd been no negative reactions to the food I had given them, but I had no idea what they had previously been accustomed to and I didn't want to cause them problems in their weakened state. Now I had seen how difficult it was for the old man to extend his limbs, I was keenly aware of how difficult and messy things were likely to become if the food upset his stomach.

The old woman's fever had abated by the time the soup was cooking and she was sleeping calmly. The old man was shaking and becoming more feverish. One was improving as the other went downhill.

I guessed there was some way to go before either of these two was truly on the road to recovery. It was going to require patience and constant monitoring. I wondered if the sorcerer was watching and whether the changes in their condition would prompt him to put in another appearance. I had been considering him while I was hacking at the anthill and was now convinced he was somehow keeping an eye on this place and my activities. He might have accepted me so far, but there was no guarantee he would do so unconditionally or indefinitely.

Darkness came before the food was ready. By the light of the hurricane lantern, I looked at the old man who was now shuddering with the fever. I managed to get him to swallow two anti-malarial pills and a little water, but it was not easy and he was in no condition to take any soup. His eyes were wandering and unfocussed and he had become unresponsive to my requests and actions. I wrapped the blanket around him and made sure he was well supported in case the shaking made him topple over, and then turned my attention to the old woman.

She woke up when I lifted her into a sitting position. Slowly she focussed and looked at me directly. I wondered what thoughts were going through her mind. Coming out of a severe fever and finding a bearded white face looming over her, even if it was offering water, must have been a major surprise. Even so, she opened her mouth to drink and, after swallowing once, extended a scrawny hand from the folds of the blanket and took the mug from my hand.

The soup was now cooked and ready to eat. I removed it from the fire, tipping a little into an enamel bowl to cool. The smell was enticing and made me feel hungry. When I passed the bowl to the woman, she had difficulty holding the spoon. Since she was willing to try and feed herself I tipped away the last of the water in the mug and replaced it with soup. She accepted the mug but stared at it for a long time before raising it to her mouth, as though considering whether it was safe to eat. I made several eating gestures but still she stared. It was only when I used the spoon and put some in my own mouth that she accepted and began to drink it. She took her nearly an hour to consume the half-mugful I had given her.

IT WAS ANOTHER LONG NIGHT. The hours after sunset were punctuated by the intermittent yipping of a patrolling jackal calling to its mate and, in the distance, the hooting laugh of a hyena. The sounds kept me looking towards the door, half expecting that vile animal to appear again. But there was only darkness.

As before, the shadow was deep and intense inside the stick hut, but outside ten billion stars populated the clear night sky and enabled me to see some distance, even before the thin waning moon broke free of the horizon. Once again I kept the cooking fire burning, but this time I didn't light any other fires to deter night visitors. I hadn't collected enough wood for this and wasn't going to wander around in the dark looking for more. I would have to devote part of the morning to collecting a supply. Now I regretted not having bought a sack of charcoal when I had had the opportunity, back in Guinea two days earlier.

Was it only two days? Time had seemed irrelevant before and I wondered why its passage should surprise me now.

Nothing had changed much by morning. The old woman was slowly recovering, her bouts of fever less frequent and much less intense. The old man, however, was slipping further into its grasp so I loaded him up with a stronger dose of pills and poured as much water into him as he would take. There was no point trying to make him eat while he was like this, but the old woman displayed some appetite when she woke up.

I made sloppy millet porridge for breakfast, loaded it with sugar and gave her a cupful to suck on. When I came back to look, she had finished it all and was asleep again, half sitting and propped against the corner pole of the hut.

I spent an hour collecting firewood and made a pile that I estimated would last several days. We only needed fuel for cooking and for a couple of night fires to warn off inquisitive animals, so it should suffice. At least we didn't need fire for warmth.

After the chores, I went back to my excavations under the Land Rover. I'd made real progress the previous afternoon but there was still a lot of digging to do before I could begin work on the engine. The inner part of the anthill was much softer than the well-baked exterior so it shaved down much more easily. By midday, the ground under the engine was flat with clear space in which to work.

I checked the old people, made myself some flat bread for lunch, then got out my tool box and sorted out the spanners I would need. The bottom of the engine was very dirty. Oil-soaked dust was heavily encrusted over all the nuts I needed to undo to get the sump off. One side of the sump had been comprehensively crushed. As I suspected, there was a split along the left side, about two inches long. This must have been where the gush of oil had come out when I hit the anthill. The angle the metal had been bent into had made hot oil spurt upwards onto the exhaust manifold. I had been lucky that the whole thing hadn't caught fire. Had that happened, it would have burned the whole vehicle, along with all my medicines, water supply, food and equipment. I had always been reasonably competent at living off the bush with very few resources, but that would have been an extreme challenge and I wouldn't have been much help to the people in the stick hut.

This thought made me go back and see how they were getting on. The old woman was awake so I heated up some water, added milk powder and gave her it to her with a small piece of the flat bread I had made for my own lunch. I showed her how to soften it to eat by dunking it in the warm milk. She got the idea quickly enough and I left her dunking bread and sucking it with her almost toothless gums. It would get some food and moisture into her and was something she could do for herself, even if she was weak.

The old man was still shuddering with fever and his temperature was high. I found a thermometer in the first aid kit and checked: it was 103 degrees Fahrenheit. No wonder he was shaking. I managed to get him to take a little water but mainly had to hope that what he had drunk in the last twenty-four hours would be enough to see him through until it eased. When the fever subsided, I would try and get him to drink more.

The situation was still critical. Both these two were on the brink. I was beginning to understand what doctors in emergency rooms must feel, seeing patients slip away despite their best efforts. To make the feeling more intense, they had all sorts of resources and other people to help them. I had a limited first aid kit, my wits and the questionable support of a sorcerer with whom I had yet to establish a channel of communication.

BY MID-AFTERNOON, I was back underneath the Land Rover, chipping away at the encrusted dirt, trying to locate the bolts that held the sump on. It was sweaty work and my hands became slippery with all the oil, causing me to drop the spanner and skin my knuckles against the sharp edges of the torn metal. I also managed to drop several of the studs as I withdrew them and had to spend time scrabbling around in the gritty remains of the anthill trying to find them. I would need them if I managed to mend this sump well enough to put it back on.

By the time the light started to fade, I had removed just over half of the sump studs. I stood up, rubbing my hands with bits of crumbling anthill to remove as much of the oil as I could before searching the back of the Land Rover for rags and a can of petrol to clean my hands properly. After that I could wash with soap and water from the big tank, but I was conscious that it was necessary to save this. There was no knowing how long it would have to last and I didn't fancy having to hike miles with a jerry can in search of water. That's one of the bugbears of life in the bush for so many communities, where women often have to make round trips of six or eight miles, sometimes several times each day, carrying sixty-pound loads simply to keep their families supplied with water.

Water supply was, after all, one of the prime reasons why I was here.

DURING MY THIRD NIGHT in the stick hut, things took a dramatic turn for the worse as far as the old man was concerned. His fever suddenly escalated. Where one moment he had only been hot and clammy, the next he began shuddering and his body was wracked by spasms. He toppled from his sitting position and continued to twitch like a stranded tortoise, with his legs in the air. I tried to straighten him out so he could lie down, but his muscles were too cramped and when I rolled him gently onto his side he remained in a foetal position, twitching erratically, perspiration streaming from his body. It was a good thing I had managed to pour all that water into him before if this was what was going to happen. I wondered if this was only fever or if he was having a fit.

The old woman was awake when it happened. She watched though blank eyes, seeing, but giving no sign that she understood what was happening. I wondered what was going on behind those tired eyes. They must have seen so much over the years. Had she seen this before? Was this the look of resignation because she had seen the game played out to its conclusion on previous occasions?

I checked the man's temperature again. It was 104.5 degrees. I wondered how long he could survive like that. Unable to think of an alternative, I poured water into the enamel bowl I had used for soup, pulled back the blanket and sat bathing his forehead, face and shoulders. It occurred to me that this was not enough, so I tipped water all over his shirt, hoping evaporation would cool him. It was a warm night and the cloth soon dried, so I repeated this while continuing to bathe his face and neck. It was all I could do until the spasms stopped as he was so tightly wound up that he wouldn't be able to swallow, even if I had been able to get him upright long enough to get a cup to his mouth.

It was a very long night.

The fever broke in the early hours, when the nocturnal chorus had died down and the patrolling jackals had retired. The old man subsided into deep sleep. He was so still it seemed more like a coma, but by the dim light of the hurricane lantern it was difficult to be sure. When his temperature dropped to a hundred degrees, I covered him with the blanket, rolling part of it up beneath his head to keep it slightly elevated.

The old woman had dozed off, but the moment I started moving to do anything around the old man, her eyes opened and she watched me intently. In the dim light of dawn, I could see new focus and interest in her eyes and this cheered me up. She was over the fever and would now recover. At least, I hoped this was so, but I had seen how quickly things could change. In her weakened state, there was no certainty yet.

As soon as it was light enough, I prepared her some more milky porridge. If she could take in enough food and water to give her energy, she might still have a chance.

After a night of dramas, I was tired myself and almost reluctant to get back to mending the Land Rover, so as soon as the old woman had been fed, I lay down on the floor of the stick hut and went to sleep. I must have slept for several hours for it was late morning and the sun was high when I woke.

The old woman was asleep and the man was as I had left him, curled on his side, motionless with several flies dancing around his face and ears. These provoked not even the slightest reflex from him and made me wonder if he had died while I slept. I reached over hurriedly to search his neck for a pulse.

He was still alive, although his pulse was erratic and his skin was clammy and cold.

FOR THE REST OF THE DAY, I alternated my time between the stick hut and lying under the Land Rover, trying to remove the last of the bolts from the sump. Some were badly corroded and it was difficult to get any tools to bite tightly enough to turn the studs. Late that afternoon I managed, finally, to remove the last one. I put these studs in an empty food tin but, dragging myself from under the vehicle, my elbow knocked the tin over and spilled most of them into the dust.

It was too dark to see what I was doing and it would be easy to miss one. Cursing at my own clumsiness, I decided to leave them where they were and deal with the problem in the morning. Now I was tired, hungry and aware that I had neglected the two old people for hours. I wiped the grease from my hands with a petrol soaked rag and used some of my precious water and soap to get them clean.

THE OLD WOMAN WAS still asleep. The old man still lay on his side, curled up like a small child. But where his skin was cold and clammy last time I had checked, now it was burning hot and his pulse was racing. This did not look good, but at least the pulse was strong. I sat him up, pushed some pills into his mouth and held a cup of water to his lips. Initially there was no reaction but after a few moments he opened his mouth and sucked hard. Almost half the cupful disappeared and I had to pull it away in case he choked. I poured the rest of the water into his mouth slowly and laid him down again.

The old woman woke when I touched her wrist, turning her head to look at me. Her vision was clearer and curiosity showed in her face. Taking this as a good sign, I helped her sit up and gave her water and more anti-malarial pills.

The hurricane lamp needed more paraffin, so I refilled it before making food. Since the old woman seemed slightly better, I hoped she might be able to eat something more than thin soup or gruel, so I made a small pot of millet porridge, cooked a chopped onion and mashed a small tin of corned beef into it. As a new variety of corned beef hash this wasn't my best creation, but it was edible and I at least was hungry after my day's labours.

When it came to it, the old woman was not up to feeding herself and I had to spoon the hash into her mouth, but at least she accepted and swallowed it. Perhaps it was my 'one for you, one for me' approach that convinced her to accept it as I fed myself alternate spoonfuls. I wasn't going to feed her something I wouldn't eat myself.

All the time she watched me carefully and again I wondered what was going on in her mind. She was much clearer now and, although she still had a temperature, her fever had not returned. I assumed her thought processes might again be whatever was normal for someone of her age, but I wondered briefly if senility had already begun before the fever attacked her and whether she really understood what was happening. It could be very frightening to return to rational thinking only to discover oneself being attended by an unfamiliar white man. She might never have seen a white man and would think I was a ghost or a spirit, there to harvest her soul.

Without knowing if she understood, I began to talk to her quietly in French, telling her she had been sick and I was helping her to get better. I told her the old man had a severe fever and I was doing the same for him. When I mentioned the man, her eyes flicked towards where he lay and back to me, watching me even more intently. I hoped this meant she understood what I'd said. But unless she spoke, I had no means of knowing.

Every hour I sat the old man up and tried to get more water into him. The shaking caused by his fever meant as much got spilled as swallowed but I had to be content with this. In between times I sat and dozed. The insects were more active tonight so I brought a few embers from my cooking fire inside and made a small smoky pile on the floor, piling green leaves on to keep a haze of smoke in the air. Some of the leaves smelled quite pleasant, but one or two were acrid and made the old woman cough and frown at me. I swiftly removed these, throwing them outside. A slight nod from the old woman's head told me this was the right thing to have done. It made me realise she must have known what the leaves were. Had she been able to talk, she could have told me which ones to use.

Familiar with life in the bush I might be, but it was things like this that made me appreciate how little I really knew and how much there was to learn. I marvelled at the capacity of people like this to survive so long in such a hostile and complex environment. Their recovery had become very important to me now and I so hoped one of them would speak a language I could understand so I might learn a little from them.

At dawn the old man's condition had not improved. I managed to push more pills into his mouth and again he spilled most of the water I offered but he took just enough to get the pills down. His temperature was still 104 degrees. How long could he carry on like that? Surely it must be doing some terrible damage?

I made a fresh pot of porridge and mixed up some milk for the old woman. She seemed to like this, holding the cup with a much steadier hand this morning. It was a good sign and gave me renewed hope. Perhaps she really was recovering, although she was obviously very frail and lapsed easily into sleep.

AT THE LAND ROVER, my first task was to collect the sump studs that had spilled in the dust the previous evening. I was one short and spent a fruitless half hour scrabbling in the dirt looking for it. There was no sign of it and eventually I gave up, deciding that I would have to find a spare bolt from somewhere when the time came to reattach the sump. Now I needed to get the mangled container off the bottom of the engine and start bashing it back into shape and mending it. That promised to be a major task.

Removing the sump was not as easy as I had expected. With the retaining studs removed, it should have been relatively easy to prise it free and let it drop clear. It didn't look as though any of the crushed area had become entangled with the working parts inside. Without being able to see it, I could only hope nothing inside had been cracked or broken by the impact. Whatever had happened had stopped the motor rather abruptly so I couldn't be sure of anything until the innards were exposed.

After another fruitless half-hour trying to prise the sump off, I finally realised why there had been one stud missing when I had counted them: it was still holding the sump onto the bottom of the engine. Once it was removed, the battered casing fell away easily and I was able to inspect the oily mechanism within. Everything looked bright and clean and there was no obvious sign of damage. Without dismantling it all and inspecting each piece, there was no way to be sure, but that was a workshop job and not one to do lying on my back in the bush over the remains of a termite castle. I would have to take it on trust and anyway, unless I could repair the sump, it didn't matter as the engine wouldn't run.

I made a cover with a sheet of plastic and string to keep the exposed engine parts clean. Once it was securely in place, I collected my tools and climbed to my feet. It was good to be out of that cramped space.

Examining the battered sump revealed not only a massive dent but a jagged split two and a half inches long. When the whole thing had been bashed back into shape, this would have to be sealed or we were going nowhere.

7 ~ Exploration and discovery

THE OLD WOMAN WAS AWAKE when next I looked into to the stick hut. She accepted a cup of water and watched me tend the old man. The fever had progressed. Now, with his skin cold and clammy, he was shivering constantly. I wrapped him more closely in the blanket, fed him more pills and water and laid him down again. Time felt like it was running away; how long could this go on?

It was approaching midday so I decided to make more flat bread and went outside to light the cooking fire. As I bent over the grate, my nostrils were filled with the awful stench of hyena. I whirled round. The animal was nowhere to be seen, but the sorcerer was standing behind me, peering in through the doorway.

How had he sneaked up like that? Even if he moved silently, the approaching smell was something that should have warned me – or could he turn that on and off like a light bulb to suit his needs? And why had he appeared at this moment?

"The woman is recovering," I told him in French as I stood up, "But the old man has a bad fever. It is lasting too long and does not respond to the medicine I've given him."

The sorcerer ignored me, going into the hut to examine the two old people himself. I moved to where I could see and watched him from the doorway as he leaned over and placed a hand on the woman's forehead. She was awake and stared at him with a blank look, the interest I had seen earlier absent from her gaze. From the depths of his own shambolic clothing the sorcerer produced an amulet which he tied round her neck. Then he turned his attention to the man.

The old man lay curled under his blanket, shivering. The sorcerer laid a hand on his shoulder and the shivering stopped. He sat like that for several minutes, neither of them moving. It was as though the sorcerer was pumping strength into the old man through his hand. When he removed it, the shivering began again, but less severely.

The sorcerer had noticed the ash of the smouldering leaves I had used to keep the night insects at bay and traced his long forefinger through the debris, lifting it to his nose to sniff the ash. His face gave no indication of what he thought as he rose gracefully to his feet and walked out of the hut. He strode off into the bush without a backward glance. Despite the open country he vanished from view within seconds. It was as if he had evaporated.

Not sure what to think, I went back to lighting the cooking fire and soon had twigs burning with bright flames. The flat iron plate I used to make flat bread went on top to start heating while I mixed flour and water and made dough. The moment I slapped the first chapatti onto the plate to cook, the sorcerer returned.

He removed a stick from my fire and took it into the hut. Casting a pile of very small twigs on top of last night's ashes, he applied the burning brand. The fire soon caught and he pulled a bundle of herbs from his clothing and began introducing selected leaves to the flames, chanting softly as he did so.

He kept up his chant for ten minutes or so, adding new leaves every so often, sometimes singly, sometimes in bunches. I watched in fascination, noticing that he used several different kinds of leaves. Some I recognised, but others were unfamiliar. It was the fresh young citrus leaves that surprised me as I hadn't seen citrus trees in the area, but their aroma when heated was distinctive. They made the place smell a lot better than our visitor did and their pungent aroma was strong even over his powerful pong.

My first chapatti was cooked by the time he had finished his ritual and I had put another on to cook. As the sorcerer emerged from the hut I tore the first piece in half and offered a piece to him. He looked at it for a moment, then accepted it and held it to his nose, watching me all the time with his piercing yellow eyes.

I bit into my own piece of bread and chewed, trying to look unconcerned while in reality speculating wildly about what he was thinking.

In his other hand, he held out a small bunch of leaves and offered them to me with a slight lift of his head. I took the leaves and looked at them. Definitely citrus, and by scraping my thumbnail across one I released the pungent aroma. The sorcerer raised his arm in the direction of the Land Rover and then raised his finger and pointed to indicate that they had come from further away in that direction. With a flash of insight, I realised that the bright green trees I had seen in the distance from Land Rover's roof were the source of these leaves.

"*Chercher encore.*" The sorcerer's voice was rasping and caught me by surprise because it was so unexpected. I needed no further explanation; his meaning was clear.

The smell of scorching chapatti made me look away to turn it over and stop it burning. When I looked up the sorcerer had vanished.

That visit had been the most bizarre medical consultation I had ever witnessed. That it had been a medical consultation was in no doubt, for he had examined both patients carefully. He had prescribed and dispensed an amulet for the old woman and had fumigated them both with special leaves and herbs burned over a new fire. When I looked inside to make sure the embers were not likely to set anything else on fire, there was no sign of any ash. His fire had consumed everything and he had brushed aside the ash, if indeed there had been any. There was nothing to show where the little fire had been. Now he required more orange leaves and he had told me where to find them.

After a quick check on my two patients and the dispensation of more water, I went back to the Land Rover and collected a goat skin bag with a good knife, a machete, a saw and some lengths of thick string. If I was going to make an expedition to collect leaves, I might as well gather more wood and collect other things I was going to need to repair my vehicle.

To bash the dented sump straight, it would need to be heated. My cooking fires had been minor affairs, using only a few sticks and twigs for fuel. But to heat that metal pan enough to make it workable would require much greater heat. To get a fire hot enough for that needed substantial bits of wood to fuel it. Where there were trees, there should be large bits of wood, my reasoning said.

It took more than an hour to walk to where the green trees stood; the ground was deceptive and they were further away than they appeared. I crossed fifteen small streambeds before I was even halfway there. As I approached the grove, the scent of oranges began to permeate the warm afternoon atmosphere. At first it was just a faint aroma that was quite pleasant after the dry dusty smell of the open bush. It grew stronger and stronger the closer I got.

The sound changed too. There was a slight humming in the air. I paid no attention to it at first, but as I came within a few yards of the grove, I realised many of the trees were in bloom and had attracted bees. I wondered if the bees were in kept hives or whether they were wild swarms. Either way, I was surprised not to see people about as most Africans love honey and will take terrible risks to life and limb to get even small amounts. But there was nobody here: the place was deserted.

Orange trees are strange plants that can bear flowers and fruit at the same time. This was soon visible here. Most of the trees showed patches of blossom; little clusters of small white stars, vivid against the contrasting darkness of the foliage. Where the bushes in the surrounding countryside looked dull and dusty, the leaves of these trees retained their sheen and looked vigorous, healthy and fresh. Most were laden with fruit as well as blossom and the ground beneath them was littered with oranges that had already ripened and fallen. Why had nobody harvested the fruit and taken it to market?

I wondered again why there were no people about. It was almost unheard of to stop anywhere in Africa and not have an audience within a few minutes. I'd been here two days and, apart from the old folks in the stick hut, the only person I'd seen was the sorcerer. I wasn't sure if he counted as a person and there were moments when I wondered if he had actually been a figment of my imagination.

Thinking a piece of fresh fruit would be pleasantly refreshing after my dusty walk I chose a ripe orange and twisted it from the tree. The fresh juice trickled over my fingers as I cut it with my knife and I felt the saliva welling up in my mouth. With this expectation of pleasure, its taste came as a complete shock. It was incredibly bitter, yet sour at the same time. It made my mouth pucker. I spat it out urgently, reaching for my water bottle. It took several large gulps of water to wash that harsh sensation from my mouth and still its memory lingered on my tongue for a long time afterwards.

I tried another but it was just as bad. As I handled the fruits, I became aware that their skins were particularly aromatic and oil from the pores was soon all over my hands. Wiping my hands over my face left me with the scent of oranges wafting in front of my nose for the rest of the afternoon. I wasn't sure if there was anything else that could be done with them, but piled a few oranges into my goat skin bag to take back to the stick hut anyway.

Leaving aside my disappointment about the oranges, I began to harvest bunches of fresh leaves. I made sure to include some sprays with blossom on them, in case they were of use to my medical adviser, as I had dubbed the sorcerer. Then I set about looking for fallen branches. I wanted a large bundle of stout sticks to make a hot fire for tempering the sump pan before trying to beat it straight.

The sun was already inclining towards the horizon by the time I had finished. I wasn't going to be back at the Land Rover before dusk. I hoisted the bundle of logs onto my head, stooped to pick up my bag of oranges and leaves, and began the long return walk. I had slashed a few bushes and deliberately scuffed the dirt on my way out and now looked for these signs to lead me back. The marks were easy enough to see in daylight but in the gloom, I soon became unsure of my direction. It looked as if I could be wandering around all night without the faintest clue where I was going, but the faint smell of word smoke on the night air gave me a clue. After half an hour, I recognised a pair of bushes I had decimated in a previous foray after firewood and soon afterwards I found the stick hut. When and how I had passed the Land Rover I had no idea.

When I reached the hut I got a surprise, for it was not merely the smell of embers that had led me in. My fireplace was brightly aflame with a pile of fresh wood lying beside it and a pot of liquid heating. Beside the fire lay several bunches of dried leaves, clearly put there by a human hand. It looked as if the sorcerer had taken over my cooking fire to brew a potion. I lit the hurricane lamp and peered into the pot, wondering what was in the cloudy green brew and hoping it was helpful and medicinal and not purely magical.

I didn't have long to examine it before the sorcerer appeared at my elbow as abruptly as before. Taking the fresh leaves from my hand, he began stripping off the small tender ones and added a dozen or so to the simmering pot. He sniffed at the blossoms but set them aside and picked up a stick to stir his brew, sitting back on his heels as he did so.

When I tipped the fruit from my goat skin bag, the sorcerer seized one. Squeezing the fruit hard so that the skin pores popped, he rubbed the skin up and down his arms, round his face and over his exposed legs. Seeing my look of surprise, he made a thin buzzing sound like a mosquito and waved it away. He was telling me that this was an effective insect repellent, so I followed his example. After covering my own skin, I took another orange into the hut and applied some oil to the exposed parts of each of the old people. The woman was awake and watched with interest as I attended to the old man. She offered no resistance when I approached her with a fruit. She obviously understood what I was doing, and approved.

As I wiped the orange over her face she inhaled deeply, appreciating the sharp aroma with a look of sadness creeping into her eyes. Did she know that the fruit itself was uneatable? Did she long for the taste of a sweet orange? I went back outside, collected a few blossoms and tied their little stems together with a twist of grass. The sorcerer watched me with interest until I held them to my nose and sniffed. He nodded and returned to stirring and gazing at his brew. I took the blossoms into the hut and gave them to the old woman. It was becoming difficult to make out her expression in the darkness, but I could see the glint from her eyes as she lifted the small bunch to her nose and sniffed. She continued holding the blossom under her nose as I went back outside.

It was obvious that the pot the sorcerer had commandeered was going to be in use for some time. I was hungry so I headed back to the Land Rover to get another one. While looking for the cooking pot, I came across the sack of yams I had bought in Guinea a few days before and decided one of these might make supper a bit more interesting, so I took it back along with the pot.

The sorcerer was still absorbed in his brew and looked like he might be for some time to come. It wasn't only the cooking pot but the hearth that was occupied, so I brought together three more stones and made another. It only took moments to get another fire going and while the kindling burned down to coals, I cut the skin off the yam and chopped it into pieces the size of an egg. As soon as there was a good pile of hot embers I spread the yam skin over the coals with pieces of yam on top, covering it all with the iron chapatti plate. A few other stones piled around the edge and some soil brushed over to close the gaps made a good closed baking oven. I put my cooking pot on top filled with water. It wouldn't heat as fast this way as over flames, but it seemed sensible to use the heat so I could make tea when the water was hot.

When the evening flight of mosquitoes arrived, the sorcerer used orange leaves to make his fire smoky, adding a selection of his own leaves to make the smoke more intense. The air had almost no movement in it that evening and the smoke hung around us, successfully keeping the insects at bay. By waving a bunch of leaves, I was able to drift a little of it through the thin wall of the stick hut so the two old people inside were less bothered by the insects.

Squatting in front of my fire beside my enigmatic companion, I wondered again at his role. He was now behaving like a medicine man, yet when I had first encountered him he was very different and menacing. Could the change be because I had intervened to stop the old people from dying needlessly? Or had their survival been some sort of trial: if they lasted beyond a certain time, he was bound to try to help them? There were so many questions I wanted answers to, and yet I hesitated to voice any of them. In any event, I was still uncertain whether this man spoke more than a few words of any language I knew. He hadn't been very communicative himself.

As we squatted side by side in front of our fires, I looked at him more closely. The strong smell of hyena that had been so much in evidence before was almost absent now. It may have been slightly masked by the smoking leaves and the smell of his brew which was now quite pungent and smelling of liquorice, but I had the distinct feeling that the hyena smell had, in some inexplicable way, been turned off. It was as if the stopper had been replaced in a bottle of hyena-scented salts. I looked to see if there was a likely container among the accoutrements that hung among the rags and skins that clothed him, but could identify nothing. Or had I simply become so accustomed to the stink that I no longer noticed it? Given the powerful nature of that particular aroma, this seemed the least likely; I was convinced he could turn it on and off at will.

I went inside to check on my patients and give them more water and pills. As I came out the sorcerer picked up one of the oranges and dug his thumb nail into the skin. By the reflected light from his cooking fire, I could see the brief spurt of mist as the oil erupted from the damaged skin. As the oil reached the fire and ignited, a brief flare flashed across the vaporised cloud and it was gone.

The memory of that same oil on my hands and how I had rubbed it over my skin and that of the sick woman gave me a momentary flash of inspiration. If that oil was effective as an insect repellent, and if there were people living in this area who could collect it, perhaps it would be useful to them and might help reduce the risk of infection by malaria-carrying mosquitoes. This wild, unadulterated stuff might even have a commercial value.

It was an idea worth exploring.

THE SORCERER VANISHED during the night. After letting his brew cool, he had made each of the old couple swallow almost a full mug of the stuff. The woman accepted it without complaint, although I could see from her face that it must have tasted disgusting. The old man, still feverish, was less accommodating and, after a few moments, the sorcerer passed the mug to me and indicated that I should get him to drink it. It was an opportunity to push some more pills into his mouth before I held the cup to his lips. To my surprise, he accepted it and swallowed without resistance. Maybe it was the manner in which it was presented that made the difference. The thought made me look round to see if the sorcerer had noticed. He was watching me intently, but his face was inscrutable. A tickle of apprehension skittered down my spine as I turned back to the old man.

When I looked around again, the sorcerer was gone. There was only a small heap of smoking cinders where he had squatted, just inside the hut's doorway. In the entrance lay more of the smoke-producing herbs he had used the previous night. He obviously intended me to use them during the night. Was this a sign of trust? Whatever it was, I took it to mean he was satisfied with how I was looking after the old people. Otherwise he surely wouldn't have left me alone with them.

8 ~ Bush mechanics

BY DAWN THE OLD MAN'S fever had abated and he lay sleeping peacefully, so I left him undisturbed. The old woman was awake before me. She reached out a hand for the mug of sweet tea even before I offered it to her. That was progress.

Although she was much better, I still dosed her with anti-malarial pills before giving her a bowl of sloppy porridge, but now she was able to use the spoon with no difficulty. She had managed to eat three pieces of baked yam the previous evening. Because she had so few teeth, I had hesitated to offer it, but she sucked and mashed the yam with her gums enough to swallow it. Now she had her appetite back she should improve rapidly.

Walking back to the Land Rover to begin repairs, it occurred to me that although I had been pouring as much water and food as I could into both the old people for more than two days, neither had yet needed to pee or ease their bowels. I wondered how long that could go on. Was either of them in discomfort as a result? I would have to consider that when I returned later.

Bashing the dents out of the sump proved to be more difficult than I expected. The oily grime was easy enough to remove from the damaged tank by using a little petrol and then burning it off. The next task, removing the dents, required an anvil and a shaped tool with which to hammer out the bottom from the inside. There was also the split to repair. It took more than two hours to carve a wooden mallet block the right shape from a piece of the wood I had collected the previous afternoon. Finding something sufficiently hard and substantial to use as an anvil was another problem. While stones were not scarce, there were none in this area large enough for the purpose and the larger ones that were lying around were soft and crumbly. I carried nothing in the Land Rover that would make a suitable substitute.

I wasted much of the afternoon wandering around the area looking for a large stone, but found nothing. The only thing that did attract my attention was a small acacia tree. It had a straight trunk almost the same diameter as the width of the sump. This sort of acacia has very hard wood. It might serve well enough as an anvil if I cut it off at a suitable height and fastened a metal plate on top.

Before doubt could dent my enthusiasm, I ran back to the Land Rover for a saw. The wood from the rest of the tree would provide fuel for heating the metal to temper the sump. I didn't have a bellows, but I did have a foot pump for the tyres; rigged up with a suitable nozzle, that should enable me to blast air into the heart of the fire like in a blacksmith's forge.

I knew the wood was hard before I started sawing, but the acacia turned out to be even harder than I expected. By the time the tree was felled, my back and arms knew they had done some hard work. It was getting dark by then so cutting up the branches into firewood would have to wait until morning.

I baked another yam that evening, mashing it and mixing in

another small tin of corned beef. The addition of a little peanut oil made it into a relatively smooth paste that anyone with no teeth could consume. The old woman obviously liked this and ate all that I gave her. The old man was still not in a condition to eat, so I had to be content with pushing pills and water into him. I added a sachet of electrolyte salts to their water in the hope it would help their recovery. They must have lost a great deal through sweating while feverish.

After three days, tiredness had been creeping up on me and I slept soundly that night. I woke to find the sorcerer prodding me with a stick and glaring at me as if I had committed a heinous crime. I whirled round in panic, thinking something had happened to one of the old people while I slept.

To my intense relief, they were both still alive. The old woman was awake, sipping a cup of water. The sorcerer must have given it to her. The old man was still asleep, but seemed more tranquil than he had been the night before.

I turned back to look at the sorcerer, wondering if he would give any indication of what he expected next, but he was nowhere to be seen. He had simply evaporated. His coming and going like the Cheshire Cat was keeping my nerves on edge, never quite knowing when, or how, he would appear again, or what his mood would be.

BASHING OUT THE BATTERED sump had to be my priority this morning so I concentrated on that. I started a hot fire using a few dry branches brought from the orange grove. Once it was burning well and some of the larger logs were glowing strongly, I dumped the damaged sump on top to heat. Among the tools I thought would be useful was an old welder's glove with which I could hold the sump when it was hot. I had been tempted to dump the glove last time I sorted out the vehicle but decided at the last moment to keep it a little longer. Now I was glad as, together with the foot pump fitted with a nozzle from a defunct inner tube, it was going to prove very useful.

It was a bright sunny day with the temperature already rising. Working with hot metal over an augmented fire was sweaty and tiring, but I made progress. By noon the sump was slightly more the shape it should have been, although far from dent free. The split was what worried me most but I had managed to bash the edges together so that it was no longer a gaping hole. The difficult bit was going to be sealing it against heat and internal pressure without welding gear.

After a brief stop at midday to check on the two old people, I returned to the task, having decided to use solder and a patch. Because of the heat and pressure involved, I couldn't be sure solder would hold when the engine was running, so the patch would need to be held tightly in place by some sort of rivets if it was to last until I could get to a proper workshop. It took all afternoon to clean the metal sufficiently for solder to stick to it and to fashion a pair of patches from corned beef tins. The metal was thin and I wasn't sure it was strong enough so I decided to put patches inside and out.

After hammering the edges of the split together on my makeshift anvil to make them as even and close as possible, I heated the sump and covered the area round the split with flux. It fizzed and hissed as it touched the hot metal and looked clean and bright. With the metal still hot, I applied solder along the length of the split, smoothing it out to cover the area of the patch with a soldering iron. When I had finished, the inside of the sump looked reasonably sound, but I got a surprise when I turned it over and looked at the outside. There were dribbles and tails of solder where it had run through the split and congealed on the outside. With more flux and the red-hot soldering iron, I applied solder to the inside curve of one patch and to the outside curve of the other.

By this stage it was late afternoon. I had been working at the task all day. It was time to stop.

9 ~ Contact

FOR SUPPER THAT NIGHT, I wanted to introduce a little variety into the meal and had the idea that vegetables might give the old people some vitamins too. So I soaked a packet of dried diced vegetables and stirred them into the millet porridge. It produced a mixture with the unappetising appearance of thick vomit but, with the addition of a little *pili-pili*, it made the taste more interesting. Fortunately, by the time it was ready to eat, darkness had overtaken me and the food's visual appearance was of little consequence.

The old woman was sitting up watching me through the open doorway as I prepared the food. Her fever was now completely gone but I continued to dose her with anti-malarial pills to prevent its return. When my *haute cuisine* was ready, I ladled some into a bowl and took it in to her with a spoon. A bony hand, looking in the dim light of the hurricane lantern like a talon, reached out from the fold of her blanket and took the bowl. Then she knocked me off my feet by saying in a remarkably clear, but husky voice: "*Merci.*"

I was so surprised I stepped backwards and banged my head

on the top of the doorway. The impact shook the whole stick hut, causing a cascade of dust, small flakes of thatch and other debris to shower down inside. I was afraid it was all going to land in the food, but the old woman's other hand had appeared to cover the bowl.

In the next few minutes, I was able to establish that the old woman spoke remarkably good French. She also told me that she felt very much better. I became so wrapped up in this discovery that I completely forgot about eating anything myself until she told me, in motherly tones, that I too should eat. I filled a bowl and sat down facing her, feeling at last that I had a companion. A thousand questions began playing tag in my mind.

Tiredness no longer mattered. The old woman's revelation opened new horizons, and gave me a new feeling of hope for her and the old man. I learned that her name was Nasia and the man was her husband. She called him Ayenu. My surmise that they had been left here to die proved to be correct, for she told me this stick hut was a house of transition, protected by the spirits and a sorcerer. From here they would not return to their village but move on to the realm of the ancestors.

I asked if my intervention had caused problems since they were expected to die. Would the spirits or the guardian be angry?

"It was meant to happen this way," she replied, going on to tell me that now she had decided not to die. With my arrival, her life received a new purpose. Her days had been extended. She said this in such a matter of fact way it seemed as if she had expected this outcome.

I asked if this was so.

"I knew you would come," was all she would say.

Not sure what this meant, I decided there would be time

enough over the next days to explore and ask questions. For the moment, I was delighted she had recovered enough to talk at all.

I told her about the hyena and the strange man it turned into. She nodded, saying this was normal. He always appeared at times like this. "He is Inyati," she explained, "The one who carries you into the compound of the ancestors."

"And what of the hyena?" I asked.

"He is also Inyati, the one who disposes of dead bodies."

This made me think. Was she telling me that the hyena would eat them when they died? Was this how her people disposed of their dead? I suddenly realised how little I knew about the people in this corner of Mali. I wasn't even sure what tribe they belonged to. I wanted to ask so many questions but Nasia forestalled me.

"Inyati is a special one. He guards others like him who are about to die. He guides their souls to the ancestors' compound. He leaves nothing for evil spirits to attach to," she continued.

"And the hyena?" I asked.

"She is part of him."

This was getting confusing. It appeared that the sorcerer's alter ego was not only an animal, but a female one. It should have made sense as the female is much more dominant among hyenas. They are peculiar creatures that defy many of the conventional norms of the animal kingdom, but at that moment this didn't register in my mind.

After an hour or so, when we had finished eating, Nasia lapsed into sleep. My enthusiasm on discovering that we could talk to one another had made me forget she was still recovering from a life-threatening fever. She was very old and still fragile.

I turned my attention to Ayenu and discovered he had soiled himself, so I spent some time cleaning him up and making sure he drank more water. It wasn't a pleasant job, but I couldn't leave him like that. It would attract flies.

Once he was clean and laid down to sleep again, I brought some coals from the fire and used the last of the sorcerer's leaves to fill the stick hut with smoke and keep the night insects at bay.

By the time I leave here, I thought, I shall be well kippered.

It may have been my excitement at discovering the Nasia could talk to me, or it may have been the effect of a long, hot day's hard work, but I slept badly that night. Dawn found me listless and with aching muscles. I was keen to talk with Nasia again but also needed to get the Land Rover mended. While my time here was proving to be an interesting interlude, other people would soon be expecting me back in Bamako and places beyond. Nevertheless, I couldn't just leave, even when the vehicle was working again. After they'd survived the fever, these two couldn't be abandoned here. I would have to make sure they would be cared for. But how?

I had no idea where their families were, nor why there was nobody here to look after them. This was an unusual situation in Africa, where family and community bonds are all important and unbreakable. There was clearly more behind their presence in this isolated hut than I had so far discovered.

10 ~ Up and running

I SPENT THE MORNING completing the repairs to the sump. The solder along the split looked as strong as it could be, but I was worried that with pressure from inside when I started the engine, it would split again. The two corned beef tin patches, one on the inside and the other outside, were supposed to prevent this. To keep them in place, I drilled nine small holes around the outside edge of the inner one and used small self-tapping screws to fix it to the sump, hammering their ends flat outside like rivets. I made corresponding dents in the outer patch to accommodate the resulting lumps and still let it lie flush to the metal, and then I did the same thing from the outside, this time drilling through both patches. With the two patches firmly secured, I flowed solder between the patches and the sump after heating it over hot coals. That finished the flux and solder, so I had to accept that this was the best I could do. It would either work or it wouldn't, in which case I had a long walk ahead.

At noon, I returned to the stick hut and gave Nasia some soup. Ayenu's condition had improved, so I sat him up and fed him a little soup as well. In all his writhing about under the effects of the fever, he had managed to scratch his face against one of the rough sticks supporting the hut. He now had a raw patch on his cheek that the flies kept bothering. I brought the first aid kit from the Land Rover, cleaned the wound and applied a clean dressing. After that the flies left him alone. He looked a sorry sight with the large white patch on his cheek, but his eyes were brighter and he watched everything, as he had when I first arrived.

That afternoon I refitted the sump to the Land Rover. It took most of the afternoon as I had bashed the rim slightly out of shape during my repairs and had to bend it carefully back into shape to line up with the stud holes and avoid splitting my soldered repair. Well before sunset, I brought out a gallon can of oil and refilled the engine. It could sit overnight and I'd look underneath in the morning to see if anything had leaked before trying to start it.

I went to prepare supper feeling I had achieved something that day.

NASIA WAS AWAKE WHEN I returned. She had heard all the banging and asked what I had been doing. I explained how my vehicle had been broken when I hit the anthill and that was why I was here and how I had been mending it.

"You were brought here," she said.

"No, I hit the anthill and broke my Land Rover. I found your hut when I was looking for help."

"You were brought here," she repeated.

"Well, I did see a hoopoe," I conceded, "and followed it to try and have a look at it."

"Hoopoe?" she asked.

"A pink bird with a crest that says 'hoo-poo-poo' and flies with floppy wings."

"That is the one who calls men onwards."

"I have heard of this before," I told her. "In Nigeria, a country far to the east of this place, they call it *sokago*, the wandering sickness."

"We know this name. But the bird also leads those who are called. You were called."

"Does the bird know why a man is called?"

"No. It merely calls and leads the one it is instructed to bring."

"And you say this bird brought me here?" I asked.

The old woman merely nodded with a faraway look in her eyes. She said no more.

It was obvious this conversation was at an end, but it gave me a lot to think about. I busied myself with food preparation, opting for mashed yams again, partly because I had a whole sack of them in the Land Rover and also because they were not common on this region and the old woman had clearly enjoyed the last one. It took about half an hour to prepare and cook. When it was well mashed, I wondered if I should put some *pili-pili* in it to add taste. I knew a lot of the food in this region was hotly spiced, but I was concerned that too much chilli might upset stomachs that had clearly seen little food in recent weeks. I asked Nasia if she liked *pili-pili* in her food.

She looked puzzled so I brought the jar of fine red powder over and showed it to her under the lamp light. She still looked puzzled so, opening the jar, I tipped a little onto the palm of my hand and showed it to her. She dipped a finger in it and put it in her mouth. Her smile when the heat hit her taste buds gave me my answer.

Not sure about Ayenu, I pointed to him and raised my eyebrows. The old woman smiled again and said: "He will eat anything, that one."

Fair enough. I shook a full teaspoonful into the pot of yam and stirred it in thoroughly, leaving the pot over the heat to thicken a little more before it was ready.

We ate well that evening. I felt it had been a good day.

In the darkness after our meal, I asked Nasia how she had learned French. She told me that as a girl she had been employed as a household servant by a colonial officer who was in charge of building a long iron road. Mighty wagons had rolled along this road in long strings. There was a huge black monster belching fire leading the way.

"The railway?" I asked.

"Yes. Some said it went all the way from Bamako to the great water in the sunset."

"That is true. It is still there today and I have travelled along it," I told her.

"How many weeks does it take?" She was inquisitive and I wondered how long ago she had seen the railway.

"It only takes two days, but it travels much faster than men walk," I told her. "How old were you when you saw this?"

"I had seen seven summers when Madame Bechault took me to work in her house. I worked nine summers more for her, until she died. After that I ran away to hide in the bush because someone said I had poisoned her."

"Why would anyone say that?"

"Because I knew about medicines and plants. Madame had taught me."

"Do you know what year that was?"

"I have a paper." She pointed to a broad upturned pot that had not attracted my attention before. I lifted it and found another wide pot beneath, with a wooden lid jammed tightly into its wide throat. When I handed this to Nasia, her clawed fingers scrabbled to remove the lid but could not get enough purchase. I offered her my knife to prize it out but she shook her head. "It must be pulled out with the fingers alone," she said.

I was about to offer her a hand when she managed to lever the wooden plug free. She pulled out a fold of yellowed paper and handed it to me. It felt bulky and consisted of a number of sheets which were obviously very precious to her. I unfolded them carefully. There were seven sheets in all.

The first five sheets surprised me for they were not what I expected at all. They were pages removed from a book; not just any book, but a book of botanical illustrations. They were beautiful etchings, each showing the leaf, flower, stem and root of a different plant. They were old and had been hand-tinted, the colours standing out clear and bright, even under the yellow glow from the hurricane lantern. I stared at them in amazement, wondering where they had come from and eager for daylight so I could examine them properly.

The sixth sheet was a letter. It certified that Nasia Ingamani was employed by Madame Bechault, Eloise, as a housemaid, and that queries about all matters concerning her should be addressed to her employer. The ink had faded slightly with the passage of time but it was still quite legible. It was dated 3rd December 1896. If, as she had told me, she was seven years old when this letter was given to her, it made her eighty-four now. No wonder she looked so old and shrivelled. She was almost an antique!

If I had been surprised by the first papers, it was nothing to what I felt as I turned over the last one. It was a folded sheet torn from an English newspaper. Bordered in black, it announced the death of Queen Victoria and showed a photograph of her funeral procession. Unfortunately the sheet was incomplete. The masthead and date were missing and there was no way of knowing if this was an original English paper or from a colonial edition. The quality of the paper suggested it might be the latter. Questions by the dozen filled my mind.

"Do you know what this is?" I asked.

"The great queen died," Nasia replied. "It happened when I was a little girl. I kept that picture when my mistress died, to remember them both."

"But this was the English queen. Do you understand the words?"

"No. The picture is enough. It is good to honour a queen like that."

"Do your people have funerals like this where everyone comes to pay respects?"

"For most people we do. Not for me or for Ayenu. We will have only Inyati because we are different."

Did she mean that she and Ayenu were sorcerers too and so had to take another route to the next life? I couldn't ask this question directly but enquired: "Does this you mean you are special, like Inyati?"

"Like him but not like him," she said, her face twisting into a slight smile. "He is a sorcerer. I am one who sees the future. Ayenu is one who heals."

"Was Ayenu treating you for the fever?"

"No. It was not permitted."

"But..." The words died on my lips as I realised that although this was a normal fever and had responded to good medicine, they had seen it as the final throw of the dice and expected no cure. Nasia had seen their future and they believed that this was how their lives could end. There was no point in fighting that. If someone else – me – came and intervened, so be it, their end would not be now. Otherwise the sorcerer was there to see them on their way; to lead their souls into the ancestors' compound and his alter ego, the hyena, would dispose of their mortal remains. There would be no funeral to mark their passing, no wailing and crying relatives displaying their grief, no music and drums to warn the ancestors of their coming. Because of their special abilities, they were different from the rest of their people and so must follow a different path.

"Will Inyati burn this hut afterwards, when you are gone?" I asked.

"It cannot burn. Only the grass outside will burn. The hut has seen others pass this way before." She sounded almost happy at this. It gave an element of continuity. It was right that as life passed through it should not end in a blaze of fire.

By arriving and treating their fever, I had inadvertently interfered with something I knew nothing about. Such doings could have far-reaching consequences. The idea made me ask more. "Will there be a problem with Inyati because I have given you and Ayenu medicine and stopped your fever?"

"It was supposed to happen. There is no problem," she replied after a long moment's thought.

Relief flowed through me like cooling fluid pulsing along my veins. I hadn't realised how tense I had become at the possibility of retribution from the sorcerer for interfering with his business.

We talked more that night and I learned many things about this extraordinary woman's life. Ayenu woke several times and I gave him more water and pills. He made no attempt to speak, although I was sure he listened. He still needed rest.

Both Nasia and Ayenu were soundly asleep when I woke in the morning, so I left them with a water bottle and cups and went to see if the Land Rover would work. Before trying to start the engine, I crawled underneath to see if the engine had leaked. It all looked clean and dry.

The moment of truth could be put off no longer. As the key turned in the ignition, there was a loud whirring noise, and the engine roared for a moment. After a few seconds it settled down to a steady rumble. There was a faint rattle, but it was an old machine and that could have been there before the accident. Otherwise it sounded normal except for a strong smell of burning oil.

Leaving it ticking over, I crawled underneath for what I hoped would be the last time to see if my repair was holding or whether there were spurts of oil coming from the sump. It still looked clean and dry; I could only hope it would stay that way. I got to my feet, making sure I hadn't left any tools lying in the dirt. Noticing a cloud of blue smoke behind the vehicle, I walked round to the back and realised what had caused the smell of burning oil. Some must have accumulated in the exhaust as the engine was dying and had sat there for the last few days. This was burning off in the hot gasses now coming from the manifold and would soon be gone. I stopped worrying about it.

The second moment of truth was when I put the vehicle into gear and tried to move it. It had been a mighty jolt that brought me to a standstill and killed the engine and it was possible the transmission had sustained damage from the impact. I was worried the shock had reverberated right back along the drive train and damaged the back axle and I kicked myself for not having thought of this before. It was too late now.

As I released the clutch there was a brief crunching sound but the vehicle rolled forward smoothly. Thank heaven for Land Rover engineering. I don't suppose they ever considered anthills when they designed this thing, but at least they built it strongly.

I turned the wheel and drove slowly towards the stick hut, stopping just outside the ring of fetish symbols the sorcerer had left in the grass. The silence when the engine was turned off was astounding. It only lasted moments before I became aware of vigorous birdsong and buzzing insects. Crickets scraped away in the grass and the shrill call of a kite sounded somewhere overhead. I looked up and saw the bird circling, several hundred feet above me, and wondered if it was telling me off for having deprived it of a meal. Like the hyena, it too depended on other animals dying for most of its diet. Sorry mate, you'll have to go elsewhere today.

Then it dawned on me that all this noise had been absent for the last few days. Why had it resumed now?

11 ~ Reprieved and restored

THE SOUND OF THE LAND Rover had woken both the occupants of the hut. More than that, it had drawn Nasia from her bed, for I found her crawling toward the doorway. In truth it was not just the vehicle that had brought her to this, she desperately needed to relieve herself and wanted to go into the bush to do so decently. Once I understood what she needed, I picked her up and carried her a few yards into the grass, setting her down behind a large bush. She weighed almost nothing and I felt how skinny her limbs were. It was a marvel that she was alive at all, let alone able to move about. But she was a determined woman and made it plain that she required no more help. I left her in privacy and went back to the hut.

Awake now, Ayenu was much better this morning. His temperature was normal and his eyes were bright. I still gave him medicine, but he was ready for food and quite able to feed himself again. I made a good pot of porridge, adding enough salt to make it taste and set water to boil for tea. Up to now, I had been a bit parsimonious with the water but with the Land Rover working again I could afford to be a little more generous as I would soon be able to go and refill my tank from a river or well. While the porridge was cooking, I gave Ayenu a bowl of water and a cloth and indicated he should wash as much of himself as he could. He was pleased to do this, so I left him to it.

Nasia had been out in the bush for some time so I walked out to see if she was all right. I found her half way back, lying in a heap. She had tried to walk back and had fallen, knocking the breath out of herself. I carried her back to the hut but she didn't want to go back inside. She asked to sit on the ground next to the cooking fire, where I could keep an eye on her and our breakfast at the same time. Very pleased to be out in the sunlight, she raised her face to the warming rays.

When Ayenu had finished washing, he too wanted to come outside. His limbs were so stiff from immobility that he couldn't stand. Not to be deterred, he crawled out and sat in the doorway.

After breakfast, I found some liniment and massaged his limbs and joints. Like Nasia, he was mainly skin and bone and his joints felt large and knobbly.

The blanket he had wrapped around him was too warm for sitting in the sunshine, so I searched the Land Rover for some clothing I no longer used. I had a few cheap tee shirts that had shrunk badly the first time I had washed them and would no longer fit me, so I gave each of them one of these. There were also a couple of lengths of tie-died material I had bought in a Senegalese market which I decided were better used by these two, who had nothing else.

Fed, washed and freshly attired, my companions looked so much better and both were delighted with their new clothes. We hadn't yet spoken of what was to happen now, but I had more or less decided that I should take them back to their own community.

I couldn't just abandon them here with nobody to care for them. At least they would look smart when I did take them back.

As the moment for our departure drew nearer, I wondered if the hyena man was going to put in another appearance and what he would think, so I asked Nasia.

"He will not come again until it is time. You have changed that."

"But will he be cross because I have deprived him of your souls? Or because I have deprived the hyena of its meal?" I asked, still worried that there might be some form of retribution.

"Anger is not part of him. He provides a service when it is needed."

I remembered she had told me that she saw the future. What did the future hold for her and Ayenu? Would they be back here again soon? She would tell me if she wanted to, but I couldn't ask. I could, however, enquire about immediate practicalities.

"You know I shall soon have to go on with my journey, but I cannot just leave you here. Where are your own people? Do you have a village?"

"The village where we lived is half a day from here," Nasia told me.

"So how did you come here?"

"The people brought us."

"Will they come and take you back now that you have recovered?"

"They will not come."

I understood this to mean that their community considered them already dead. They had been moved to this dying house and everyone knew Inyati would leave no trace of them. There was no reason to come looking for them.

But would the community take care of them if I took them back to the village? I hesitated to ask the question, but it couldn't be avoided.

"I cannot leave you here with nobody to take care of you," I said. "And I cannot remain long myself. If I take you to the village, will the people look after you? Do you have sons and daughters there? Surely they will be pleased you recovered and have not died."

"We have many children. They will feed us." She made no comment about what they would feel about the old people not having died. It felt insensitive to push the point, despite my curiosity.

"Then I will take you there."

Nasia nodded and I looked at Ayenu to see if he had understood. He had still not spoken and I was not sure if the was able to follow our discussion.

I looked back at Nasia and asked if the old man understood. "Does he speak French?" I added.

"He hears but he says little."

She was being enigmatic again and hadn't answered either question. I decided to buy myself some thinking time by sorting out the chaos in the back of the Land Rover. For the last few days, I had been rummaging about for items I wanted without much attention to tidiness. Now it was a mess. A couple of hours spent unloading everything, repacking baskets and boxes and reloading it all brought some sense of order. When it was finished, I stoked up the cooking fire and put a pan of water on to heat for tea. It was time to make decisions.

While the water was heating, I wandered out into the bush, past where I had first noticed a fetish sign. It was no longer there.

The grass was undisturbed. There were no feathers, no seed pods and no twists of grass holding everything together. I walked round to where the other symbols had been, but found nothing. They had all vanished, including the one above the door of the hut. It was as if they had never been there. Yet I knew they had.

I looked where I had first seen the hyena for the tracks which had been so clear before. The ground was smooth, as if nothing had walked across it for a very long time. Bending down to see if the tracks had become filled in with dust it was clear that there was no loose dust. There were no tracks.

Had I imagined those as well?

No, those things had been real. The hyena and the man had been real, and Nasia had told me about Inyati. She wouldn't have talked about him in the way she had if he had just been a creature of my own imagination.

She had said he would not be angry at my interference and all these things having disappeared seemed to confirm this. He had withdrawn and would not come again until the old folk approached their end a second time. Nasia had said he had no anger in him and I understood what that meant now.

I wondered if the villagers would be so charitable and accepting when I took Nasia and Ayenu back to the village. There was the risk of all sorts of taboos being infringed. The villagers could easily resent my interference.

Well, worrying about it would get me nowhere.

I made the tea and then prepared some chapattis to see us through the day and to take me on once I had dropped them off with their own people. I didn't intend to hang around as the breakdown had already delayed me enough. Was it that, or fear of what the villagers reaction would be, I wondered momentarily.

There was no point in worrying; *que sera sera*. Waiting for the chapattis to cook, I asked Nasia about the leaves that the sorcerer had used to make his smoky fires at night.

"*Nsu*," Ayenu said before she could answer.

So he did understand French, and he could speak. I turned to ask him more and found he was struggling to get to his feet. When I asked him what he wanted, he merely pointed out into the bush and I understood that he too needed to go and relive himself. I helped him upright and then propped him against the tailgate of the Land Rover, telling him to wait a moment while I found him a stick. He looked at me blankly as if my words had been in Martian but sat slumped on the tailgate flap recovering after the exertion of trying to stand.

Machete in hand, I marched off to the woodpile beside my tree stump anvil. There must be one or two straight sticks among that lot which might suit him. It only took a few moments to find a strong five-foot branch and trim off the knobbly bits. By the time Ayenu had recovered his strength and was ready to move, I had a good stout pole ready for him. He wrapped his bony fingers round it and heaved himself upright. With me holding his other arm, we made slow, unsteady steps towards a small clump of tall grass a few yards away. As we progressed, his steps became more definite and I marvelled at the resilience and determination of this remarkable pair.

I had completely forgotten about the chapattis, but fortunately Nasia had not. When I came back I found her turning them over so that they didn't burn. She tossed her head slightly as I thanked her for this, as if to say 'You should have been paying proper attention instead of fooling around with sticks and old men who need to pee,' but said nothing. She too was made of stern stuff.

Ayenu came back under his own steam and resumed his seat on the tailgate. It was clearly easier than lowering himself to the ground.

I doused the cooking fire once the chapattis were cooked and the tea was brewed. Then I looked to see if anything had been left inside the stick hut, finding only the old flat pot with Nasia's papers in it. I brought this out and put it beside her.

As I was turning away to check the Land Rover, she asked: "Tell me about the great queen. Why did they bury her that way?"

There was to be no rushing this old lady, I realised. I would have to be patient, so I sat down beside her.

"It was a long time ago. Long before I was born, so I do not know much. But that is the way my people honour the great ones," I began to explain. "All the people crowd the street and important men from other tribes and other countries come to pay respect. They take the body in a procession for everyone to see and go to a special building where the priests make a ceremony. After that they make another procession and take the body to a holy place where it is buried in a hole in the ground beside other great queens and kings that have gone before. After that the new ruler is installed."

Sitting in the middle of nowhere, trying to explain about royal funerals to someone from a totally different culture was a surreal experience. It made me wonder if they have a queen. Would she, when she died, be left for the hyenas because she was special, like Nasia and Ayenu had been? Or did her people have a different ritual for rulers and chieftains? Was this death house a place only for those with supernatural abilities? Would the sorcerer himself one day come here, or would he simply be eaten by his alter ego? There was no way to ask these questions.

By the time everything was cleared up and the stick hut had been swept out, it was almost midday. The previous day I had burned the rags the two old folk had been wrapped in when I found them. Now there was nothing more to do.

By removing his fetish signs, the sorcerer had effectively unlocked the door. We were free to leave. I lifted Nasia into the Land Rover and slid her across to the middle seat. Ayenu insisted on climbing in himself, accepting his stick when I handed it to him and slammed the door. As I climbed into the driving seat, I found a fly whisk there. I tucked it on the shelf below the dashboard and asked in which direction their village lay. Nasia looked round, trying to get her bearings, but there was no hesitation from Ayenu. He pointed north-east, flicking his hand upwards with the finger pointing as if to say 'move on, go that way.'

The engine started smoothly and I prayed silently that it would keep going, that my repair would hold and not leak and lose all the oil. We rolled forward and left the dying house behind.

IT TOOK LESS THAN AN HOUR to find the village which was only about eight miles away. All the way, Ayenu's directions were clear and definite. He might have been old and not very mobile, but he must have walked this land extensively during his long life. With unerring skill, he guided me around every obstacle as if he was aware that I was nursing a sick machine, and brought us to the village without any trouble.

Just before the village, we came to a patch of fields that were waiting for the next rains. Old millet stalks had been made into stacks and the ground had been cleared. Some of it was already cultivated and we could see where the hoe had been wielded. Now a few scrawny chickens scavenged the ground for grubs and errant

The bush made Nasia's village almost impossible to see until you were actually in it.

seeds and a small flock of grey speckled guinea fowl scuttled about, chattering as they ran, pausing now and then to peck at something before hurrying on.

The village was difficult to see until we were almost upon it. In the heat of the day, it looked deserted, but the noise of the Land Rover soon brought people to their compound doors. At first all the attention was on me as I climbed from the cab. White men were obviously seldom seen in these parts. Indeed, Nasia had already told me that she didn't think there had been a white man here for more than forty years. Most of the people would never have seen a white man and so my arrival caused great excitement. The air reverberated with happy chatter and the clamour of greetings grew as rapidly as the crowd, everyone wanting a sight of this strange man.

Suddenly here was silence, everything stopped as if a switch had been thrown. I looked around, thinking the sorcerer who had kept surprising me at the stick hut had put in one of his spectacular appearances and stilled the crowd. But he was nowhere to be seen. Nor was his habitual companion, the scent of hyena, detectable either.

Everyone was staring at the cab of the Land Rover. A child had recognised my passengers, but they were supposed to be dead and gone to join the ancestors. Now here they were. How could this be? Ancestors did not appear like this. Something must be terribly wrong. Faces all around me showed various degrees of fear from bewilderment to abject terror. To these villagers, this was going to need a very convincing explanation and I hadn't even considered this.

Before I could do anything, Ayenu found the catch and opened the door on his side of the vehicle. Those crowding round to look recoiled as he stepped gingerly to the ground, using his new stick to hold himself upright. They knew who he was, but was he real? Was he really alive or was he a strange spiritual manifestation, a malevolent spirit come to torment them?

Their confusion was partly resolved by the appearance of another sorcerer. A tall thin man in his fifties, he wore dusty khaki shorts, a faded blue shirt and was festooned with amulets. He pushed his way through the throng. Apart from the amulets, short ruffs of raffia tied round his ankles, and bunches of small red feathers stuck in his hair, he looked relatively normal. But there was no doubting who he was, or the authority he wielded.

The crowd parted to give him passage, then coalesced around him, pressing forwards, feeling safe now that he was here to take command of the situation, to fend off evil spirits. Nobody wanted to miss any of the action.

The sorcerer stomped up and down, spinning round and walking the length of the Land Rover before coming back to stare closely at Ayenu. He said something that sounded like a challenge.

Ayenu replied with only two words. The sorcerer stamped his feet again. He did a brief shuffle and leaned past Ayenu to peer inside the cab. He didn't get time to issue a challenge this time for Nasia spoke first. I couldn't understand her words, but their tone had the sorcerer recoiling to dance on the spot as he had earlier. He can have had no doubt the old woman was very much alive.

His skipping reminded me of a dancing devil I had seen when I was down in Liberia the previous year. It made me wonder if the Poro cult reached this far north or whether it was in any way related to these people's animist beliefs.

Moving round to the other side of the vehicle, I helped Ayenu shuffle forward to sit on the front bumper beside the winch. With him out of the way, it was easy to lift Nasia out and carry her round to sit on the other side of the front bumper.

As I put her down, I asked: "Are any of these people your children?"

"My sons are here," she indicated with a toss of her head. Somehow I knew that she meant the two tall men standing at the back, seemingly distancing themselves from what was happening. Both looked very uncomfortable and apprehensive. The reappearance of anyone believed to have died was likely to have that effect on people.

"Do they speak French?" I asked.

"Akleno does."

The crowd were hushed again, waiting for their sorcerer to pronounce. He was still shuffling and muttering, stroking the amulets round his neck, absorbed by his own thoughts.

I stood up straight and in a loud voice asked: "Which of you is Akleno?"

A tall, heavily bodied man flinched, so I pointed at him and

Akleno and his family. At first he was reluctant to accept his parents back from the dead.

said: "Come and take care of your mother. Her sickness is gone. Inyati has released her."

There was a horrified gasp from the crowd of watchers. I looked down at Nasia to see if she had fallen off the bumper, but she hadn't moved. Softly she told me off. "We do not say that name. I told it to you only because you are a stranger and needed to understand."

Whoops. I would have to tread carefully to get these people's cooperation and persuade them to look after these two old folks.

"And what of this other sorcerer, does he too have a name I should not say?" I asked.

"He is Etu Ikemongoutlu. You can speak his name."

She looked up as the crowd parted and her son came reluctantly forward. "Etu understands French, but he will not speak it to you," she added quietly.

There was an exchange between Nasia and her son which

sounded, on his part, more like a rebuke than any declaration of happiness at seeing his mother restored and well. After a few sentences, he walked off and some of the crowd began to drift after him. Nobody had said a word to Ayenu since the witchdoctor had challenged him. Now he sat slumped against the radiator grille on the other side of the bumper.

"Isn't your son going to take you to his house?" I asked Nasia.

"He said I went to die. It is wrong to come back. He said I am like a *tokoli* and should have remained with the ancestors. He no longer sees me."

"Can you go back to your own hut?"

"It was burned."

It finally dawned on me that bringing them back had precipitated a series of problems which would have echoes through the village for some time to come. I was about to enquire if other members of her family would accept her into their houses when a small girl approached, holding something wrapped in a leaf. She offered this to Nasia without a word, her eyes lowered in a gesture of her dutiful respect.

The old woman accepted the package, briefly caressing the child's hand with her fingers. Unfolding the leaf, she extracted a cashew nut and popped into her mouth, nodding slightly and cooing as she did so.

The little girl's face brightened immediately, a broad smile showing bright white teeth, her eyes sparkling. She spread her arms and wrapped them round her grandmother's frail body which was scarcely bigger than her own. It was a relief to see that at least one person welcomed her back to the family fold.

After a few moments the little girl ran off, returning a few minutes later with another leaf-wrapped package which she offered to Ayenu. There were tears in his eyes as he accepted it and was rewarded with a similar uninhibited embrace when he put the cashew in his mouth. This simple action proved to the little girl that these were not *tokoli*, but her grandparents. They had merely been away from the village for a while. Now they were home. Life was normal again.

In the words and actions of the innocent we see truth. The thought made me look round at the faces of the watching villagers. The most striking was Etu, the sorcerer, who wore a look of utter confusion. The significance of this child's simple gestures was not lost on the others either. Two middle-aged women approached, chattering enthusiastically. I realised these must be the old couple's daughters who were pleased to see their parents alive and well. Welcome was evident in their voices, even though I couldn't understand their words.

My apprehension began to dissipate. Nasia and Ayenu were helped by their daughters to stand and, supported by welcoming arms, walked slowly into the village to their compound. Sadness suffused with pleasure flowed through me as I watched them go, wondering what their future held and when they would again have to face the one whose name should not be spoken. Then it occurred to me that while I had found him startling, even terrifying, they had not seen him like that. To them he had been a welcome guide.

What a contrast in viewpoint a different culture can make.

The moment was cut short by a small hand taking hold of mine and pulling me forward. It was the granddaughter who had brought the leaf-wrapped cashews, urging me to go with her. It appeared I too was invited to their home.

12 ~ Moving on

THE CHILD LED ME INTO the village to a large compound with five huts in it. The roofs were all neatly thatched, the walls smoothly plastered with mud and the courtyard was tidy. For all its neatness, the place had a feeling of life in it. Looking round, I could see an open cooking hearth, a stack of firewood and a broad pile of lumpy mud with black ash around it. This, I guessed, must have been where the old folks' house had stood before they were taken to the dying house. After the thatch and contents had been burned, the walls were helped to tumble inwards to show people and spirits alike that the occupants had passed on and no longer lived in the house. The family had been a bit premature in doing this. With her ability to see the future, I wondered if Nasia had foreseen it.

Later that evening, her daughter explained that the remains of the houses of dead folk were traditionally left like this until the rains came. Once they were soaked by rain the mud blocks could be broken up, made into new blocks and used to build a new hut for the next girl in the family when she married. I wondered how this return changed that. If they lived in a daughter's house until they finally died, would that be similarly destroyed? Then where would the daughter and her children live and how would the spirits know where to find them?

There was no party that night to welcome the two oldest members back to the family, but each of their children came in turn to see them and exchanged a few words. Some were clearly delighted and made them most welcome. A few looked uneasy; the natural order of things had been upset, they were unsure how to deal with this situation and had received no guidance from the village sorcerer. He had rapidly lost interest and wandered off after he saw Nasia's granddaughter give her the cashew. I wondered if that little girl was in some way 'special'. Or was she just a little girl, pleased to welcome back someone she loved and had missed? Whatever her attributes were, the sorcerer had been unwilling to challenge her unquestioning acceptance of her grandparents' reality.

As other family members came to pay respects, the courtyard filled up. Soon a good crowd of happily chattering people were gathered around us. Nasia and Ayenu were installed on grass mats, some yards apart, where relatives and friends could gather round and talk. Most of the time, they simply sat and watched, although I noticed Nasia had quite a lot to say to a few individuals. As far as I could see, Ayenu spoke little. He was content to sit and listen, accepting calabashes of drink when they were offered to him, but not involving himself in the conversation. Soon after dark he dozed off, unnoticed by those around him, his head forward, resting on his knees.

Food was produced and passed around. At one point, Akleno arrived, looked round the assembled family and picked me out. He came over and sat down next to me, accepting a bowl of food from one of his sisters on the way. Without any preliminaries he launched into what concerned him.

"Why did you bring them back here?" he demanded.

"Their fever had gone away. They could not remain on their own without food or water."

"The ancestors do not need food or water as we do," he snapped back aggressively.

"They are not ready to join the ancestors," I said. "Should I leave them to starve when I can feed them?"

"But they had already gone through the gateway."

He seemed genuinely upset that his parents had survived and I found it difficult to fathom why. Did their return diminish his status?

"What gateway?" I asked.

"That hut is their gateway to the ancestors' compound. Those who enter do not come back. They cannot be seen again except by their guide."

"You mean Inyati?"

He flinched and leaned away from me.

"That name is not to be spoken here! The owner of it is not of this world." He looked most uncomfortable even talking about the sorcerer and clearly feared there could be repercussions since he had been thwarted in his allotted task. Whether as man or spirit or beast, he was the eater of dead bodies and had been left hungry. "He is not one to make angry," he concluded.

Why was he afraid? Nasia had told me the sorcerer had no anger in him. He had shown me no hostility because of my actions. It struck me that she might know a lot more about this than her agitated son.

Then I realised Akleno had probably been the one who took

Nasia and Ayenu to the stick hut, not expecting them to survive the fever. He had left neither food nor water for them because they shouldn't have needed it. Now, with their return, he felt guilty. His discomfort was compounded because, without him being aware, an outsider had come along and helped them. I knew nothing of the rites of passage of these people, but guilt at not having performed one's duties properly is a universal emotion; it didn't need any knowledge of the local culture to see why he was upset.

He sat there brooding for a few minutes while I ate the spiced beans in silence.

"They only had a small fever," I said after awhile. "Strong medicine was able to cure it. They might be old, but they were not ready to join the ancestors. Any man could have thought and done as you did," I told him. "We all fear losing our parents; we are sad when they are sick like that. We try to honour them when their time comes by taking them to the gateway so that their spirits do not get left to wander eternally in the bush, lost and alone. You did what was right. But their spirits changed their minds about leaving you. That is what happened."

I hoped I wasn't pushing my luck here, but felt he needed some reassurance.

He still sat gloomily, ignoring the happy chatter all around us, so I decided to distract him with a question.

"Do you know the orange trees beyond the dying hut? Does anyone own those trees?"

"I know them. Their fruit is cursed."

"Do you know who is the owner of the trees?"

"The hornets and the ants. No man can eat that fruit."

"You say they are cursed. Is that a sacred place? Is it taboo?"

"No. You can go there but the fruit is no use, so why go?"

He didn't seem willing to converse much. Maybe he was still piqued because I had indirectly suggested he was neglectful by bringing his parents back very much alive, or maybe there was some other reason. After a while he got up and left without saying anything else.

It was long after midnight and the family was still wide awake but I was tired and needed to sleep. The tensions of the day had eased with liberal consumption of the local hooch, but now my brain and my body both needed rest. I worked my way over to where Nasia was sitting among her cronies and told her I was going to sleep in my Land Rover. I would call on her in the morning before I left the village. She nodded and turned her attention back to her lifelong friends. Evidently I had served my purpose and was no longer needed, or perhaps she knew something I didn't.

Walking through the quiet village, I wondered what other momentous events the old woman had foreseen in her lifetime.

THE SEATS IN THE FRONT of a Land Rover are not the best place to get a good night's rest. A cock crowing and the shrill voices of village children woke me. A crowd of them had gathered round the Land Rover for another sight of the strange pale-skinned visitor. Like children all over Africa, they were curious for every scrap of information that might fall their way. They would catch it and pass it on, tossing it from one to another in a babble of shrill comments as each explored the possibilities it might offer. They were curious and shy at the same time, giggling and chattering to one another for no apparent cause, but always intensely interested.

Among those surrounding me this morning, some were naked,

Village children: forever curious, a trait shared all over Africa.

wearing no more than a necklace or a string of beads around their waist, their belly buttons protruding like brown eggs from stomachs bloated by worms. Others wore threadbare shirts or scraps of cloth wound round their agile bodies, and all were barefooted. Their merry throng made me think of Western children and how they might have behaved had I turned up unexpectedly in their village. A few would probably have stared briefly, a comment might have been passed, but there wouldn't have been any of this bubbling excitement and enthusiasm, tinged with a frisson of fear because I was something new and unknown. To me, this crowd of children felt like a welcome committee.

Somewhere in the back of the Land Rover there was an old ball I had found it when tidying up. Opening the canvas cover, I climbed into the back to look for it. Little faces lined the tailgate, all curious to peer inside.

I found the ball, climbed out and bounced it several times on the ground. A burst of excited chatter turned to shrieks of delight as I hurled it high into the air. Dozens of little brown bodies raced to be underneath when it came back down. They needed no more from me as they hurtled about chasing the ball, a happy melée that was a mixture of a game of football and a mob playing tag.

One of Nasia's daughters came over offering me food. I walked back to her compound with her and found her mother sitting against the wall outside a hut. There was no sign of Ayenu and the rest of the family had dispersed about their daily tasks. I sat and ate while I talked with Nasia and her daughter, who also had a few words of French. They told me which way to go to find the nearest town where I might get help from a mechanic.

As I got up to make my farewells, Nasia took hold of my wrist. "I will see you when you come again," she said.

I wasn't sure I would ever come to this region again and began to protest that it wasn't in my plans. There was work in other places that would keep me away.

"Akleno will help you with the oranges," she added.

This made me pause. I had no intention of doing anything with any oranges. I knew from experience they were inedible and Akleno had told me they were unusable. Even the wild animals left them alone.

But there was more. "You will make the oranges work. I have seen this."

There was no arguing with that. She was a seer. This was her prophesy, however unlikely it might sound. You don't ignore pronouncements of this sort, even if you don't understand them at the time.

The old woman gave me no chance to reply, dropping my hand and closing her eyes firmly. I was dismissed.

After thanking her daughter and promising that when work brought me to this part of the country again, I would come and visit her mother, I left. The previous evening I had given her a small packet of anti-malarial pills. She promised to give one each day to Nasia and Ayenu until there were none left.

The two were back with their family and there was nothing more they needed me for. It was time to go.

THE VILLAGE SORCERER was standing in front of my Land Rover, daubing the bonnet with a sticky brown substance that smelled horrendous. Was I going to have that wafting in my nostrils wherever I drove? Curiously, despite the stink, the goo had not yet attracted a cloud of flies.

He hadn't seen me approaching so I watched from a few yards away while the sorcerer continued his ritual, uncertain of its purpose but reluctant to interfere. Something told me this was not hostile; he was not threatening me, so I waited until he had finished. Other spectators gathered. Among them was Nasia's son, Akleno, so I sidled over to him and asked if he knew what this was about.

"I bade him do this. He is mending your sick car," he said, smiling for the first time.

"That is kind. Thank you."

"You mended our sick people."

"I only did what you would have done yourself if you had the medicine. I am pleased they are well now," I said.

The sorcerer finished his blessing and managed to melt into the surrounding crowd unnoticed. It was peculiar the way these men could arrive and depart so stealthily. At least this Etu chappie didn't smell like the hyena man. He lived here in the village; I had passed his house, and nobody would have wanted him around all the time if he smelled like the other man – if man he was.

Leaving the sorcerer's goo spread across the front of the Land Rover, I shook hands with Akleno, climbed aboard and slammed the door. As I started the engine, Akleno came to the window and took my hand again. "Come again," he said. "You will be welcome."

I was about to drive off when I noticed the fly whisk lying in the dash tray. I climbed from the cab, heading once more to where I had left Nasia. "You left this," I said, holding it out to her.

"It is not mine. It was left for you," she said, pushing it away.

"You mean In...?" The name faltered on my lips.

"You should take it, and remember." She closed her eyes. The discussion was ended. I got back in the Land Rover, said goodbye again to Akleno and moved off. The village soon disappearing into the bush behind me.

There were no roads in this part of the country and precious few footpaths. For the next fifty-seven miles, I nursed the Land Rover along, constantly in fear my repair would fail and I would find myself stranded again with a split sump. But somehow it held – the sorcerer's blessing must have been powerful – and five hours after leaving the village, I drove into the little town of Ouelessebougou.

13 ~ Back to work

OUELESSEBOUGOU WAS A rundown backwater, but at least it had a mechanic equipped with welding equipment. His eyes expanded when I explained what had happened and showed how it had been mended. He shook his head, tutting, and told me it was lucky not to have ruptured within the first mile. It certainly was, I thought, glancing at the sorcerer's goo which was now covered in dust.

The mechanic was in the middle of another job and said I would have to wait my turn. Since I was keen to get it properly mended and get on my way, I offered to do the dismantling. His face said he clearly wasn't expecting customers to get their hands dirty too, but he agreed and offered a ramp so that it wouldn't be necessary to jack up the front of the Land Rover and prop it as I had before. He left me to get on with it.

Once more I found myself lying on my back beneath the engine with a cluster of curious onlookers. This time, being able to drain the oil and to work in relative comfort meant I soon had the sump removed and washed down. I surveyed the guts of my engine but couldn't see any obvious damage. I had been most fortunate.

Now I had to wait for the mechanic to finish what he was doing and whatever it was took him the rest of the day. To while away the time, I wandered round the town and visited the market, a comet tail of chattering children and occasional curious adults following my every move. Everyone wanted an opportunity to sell me something or to perform a minor service which might earn them a few francs. They were a happy, friendly crowd and nobody took offence when I declined proffered goods. It was easy to use up the waiting time, and as the sun headed down to the horizon, I returned to the workshop and was disappointed to find the mechanic still hadn't completed the other job.

He promised to do my welding first thing the next morning. There was nothing for it but to spend another uncomfortable night sleeping across the front seats and hope he was as good as his word.

The morning cheered me up because the mechanic turned out to be better than I expected. He took a quick look at my sump and

The main street in Ouolossebougou.

strode off to search for something in a pile of scrap. He came back with another split sump, marked up both with a piece of chalk and ignited his oxyacetylene torch. Bright sparks cascaded from the metal as he cut out the damaged part of my sump and a similar, but undamaged section from the other one. The new piece was slightly larger than the hole he had made in my sump but it didn't take him many minutes to trim this with a grindstone and weld it firmly in place. Being a belt and braces man, he welded inside and out. This patch, he assured me, would neither leak nor come off. I believed him.

By midday the repair was done. My engine was reassembled, filled with oil and tested. I was ready to roll. From a standpipe near the workshop, I took the opportunity to flush out and refill my 120-litre water tank and I bought ten gallons of fuel from a man who had set up shop under a huge mango tree at the edge of town with a couple of forty-gallon drums. His passing trade looked a bit thin. I was his only customer that morning. A young woman grilling corn cobs and small pieces of stringy chicken on a small charcoal brazier nearby was doing a little better. I bought lunch from her and then headed for Bamako to pick up the threads of my work. I needed to collect my telex messages and find out what had been going on while I had been out of contact.

The going was slow. I might have been travelling on roads but most were little more than tracks and had not seen a grader or any other maintenance machinery for years. It took me six hours to get back to the capital.

There I learned that one of my well-digging instructors had fallen down a well and broken his ankle, there was a new enquiry asking for advice about cleaning up a polluted water supply in Dahomey, and a string of reports had come in from the projects I had recently visited in Senegal. I also received disappointing news about the Cessna I normally used as my long-range transport. It was undergoing a major overhaul and would be grounded for a further eight weeks until a critical spare part arrived from the factory in America.

I had hoped to be airborne again on my return. Disappointed, I headed back to my base in Upper Volta with a long list of widely dispersed tasks facing me. Leaving Bamako and heading east, I went to Kofoli to find out about Agame Kuto's broken ankle and to see what was happening at the well-digging school.

I shouldn't have worried. Oyadé, the man I had recently appointed as the manager, had everything under control. Agame, for the few weeks that he would be incapacitated with his leg in plaster, was to remain at the school, manage the daily tasks there and lead the classroom work.

That night we got word that one of the students, a man from Cameroon, had been concussed when a rope broke and the steel bucket it was lifting fell back down the well and hit him on the head. Although he was wearing a hard hat at the time, he wasn't using a chin strap. The bucket knocked the helmet off his head and toppled him heavily against the concrete wall. Someone at the top hadn't checked the rope when it became frayed and a knot had come undone.

Today an accident like that would give the health and safety people apoplexy. There and then things were simpler: the man had a headache, the bucket was undamaged and the rope had been reattached firmly. The instructor on that site was now giving his whole crew lessons in tying knots.

Accidents come in threes: I wondered what the third would be. I found out the following morning.

A young American Peace Corps volunteer called Martin Pipe had recently joined the well school as an instructor. Soon after his arrival, he had been nicknamed the Baseball Kid. He loved the game and always carted a ball and bat around with him. While waiting for his students to assemble after breakfast, he decided to have a quick game. He gave one of them the bat and pitched the ball at him. The man, who didn't know what he was doing, took a mighty swing, connected with the ball and sent it straight through the driver's windscreen of my Land Rover.

It was going to be a draughty nine-hour drive home – and a good thing the rainy season hadn't started.

Arriving back in my own village, as I now thought of Anéhigouya, I received a merry welcome. I'd been away for eleven weeks and a few people had been asking if I had left for good. The Wa-Wa man was particularly pleased to see me and came scratching at my gate as soon as decency permitted, just after dusk, keen to hear my news. He was very interested in my encounter with Nasia, whose reputation he knew well, despite her living many hundreds of miles away. There must have been a network among the sorcering fraternity.

He laughed when I told him about Etu and the goo he had slapped on my Land Rover to protect it against breaking down and, when I told him how the windscreen had been smashed, said I should carry special insurance against flying objects.

"Etu's protection was for your motor, and it worked," he said, adding with a chuckle: "You need different protection against a ball."

It is unwise to argue with witch-doctors. They may not have all the answers but their logic is infallible.

PART 2

PART-TIME
PENTECOSTALISTS

The road into the forest.

14 ~ The laundry ladies

THE NEW ENQUIRY I HAD received in Bamako was from two women who had a commercial laundry business but needed a decent supply of clean water. Their current supply from the river gave only silty water. I had carried out a clean water project not far away in Togo not long before and word of this had somehow percolated though to their village. The women wanted me to do something similar for them. I went to have a look.

From Anéhigouya to Dahomey by road was a long and tedious journey. Normally I would have flown down to Porto Novo in about four and a half hours and got road transport for the last few miles but my aeroplane was grounded for a major service so I had to drive. Going the whole distance by road was altogether different. The roads in eastern Upper Volta were poorly maintained and most were only graded once a year, if that. They hadn't seen a grader since the last rainy season and travel on many stretches required four wheel drive with frequent diversions off the road to get round collapsed culverts. In places the road was missing altogether. Across the frontier, seven and a half miles from Nadioum, the long haul south through Togo was no better. The road didn't improve until I reached the blacktop at Atakpame and even this was unpredictable as the tarmac was edged erratically, full of potholes and only covered the last fifty miles approaching the coast. Only on this stretch could you drive consistently at more than twenty-five miles an hour.

The frontier crossing from Togo into Dahomey at Grand-Popo was choked with traffic. The Dahomeyan customs officers were taking a long time to process each of the hundred or so heavily laden *mammy* wagons waiting to cross. Efforts by smaller vehicles to jump the queue met with open hostility. Obstruction and delays increased; the officers imposed spontaneous penalties. Try to argue and the fines were apt to be summarily doubled. It was wiser to wait your turn or take another route.

After waiting an hour with no prospect of the situation changing, I decided to go back and try another crossing. I started to turn around but before I had completed my turn, a customs officer was knocking on the passenger windscreen demanding that I stop. He told me that having joined the queue, I had to get back in line and wait my turn.

I started explaining that I had decided not to cross today and would come back another day, but he said that would not be necessary, I could cross immediately, without any more delay. It soon transpired that he was going off duty and wanted a ride to Lokossa, the first major town after the frontier. For this he, as the senior customs officer on duty, had the authority to take me to the front of the line.

I wondered what the waiting wagon drivers would think of this, but nobody seemed concerned. It was evidently a common practice which they all recognised and accepted. I was just the lucky driver who had been randomly picked for the honour.

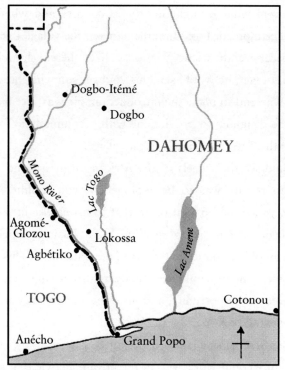

Southern Dahomey

The formalities were completed in minutes, each official at the crossing stamping my documents with a smile and only the most cursory inspection. Nobody bothered looking in the back of my vehicle.

The road as far as Lokossa had a tarmac surface and had recently been repaired. The customs officer made a point of telling me about this, saying how much better the roads were in his country than across the border in Togo. He was right, the Togolese roads were atrocious.

When we arrived at the town, he insisted on taking me to a bar and buying me a beer as thanks for the ride. It was only then that he enquired what brought me to his country and where I was going. The moment I told him the name of the village I was going to, he became enthusiastic. His cousin lived there. I should go and see him. In fact, he would send his younger son with me, to show me the way and to make the introduction. He was sure his cousin would be delighted to provide me with accommodation at a fair price as there were no hotels in the village.

I could see the wheels of the African business mind turning. Any opportunity was to be exploited. If you couldn't do that directly, you should pass it on so that someone else in the family could benefit. The act of passing on a business opportunity created an obligation to be redeemed at a later date. This ensured that some benefit would eventually return to the person who discovered the opportunity, and his esteem and status among his relatives would grow.

I also recognised that if handled carefully by me, this opportunity could work well to my advantage. Getting anything done in this part of the world depends heavily on who you know and what influence they can exert. Having this senior customs officer as my friend could pay good dividends in the future. I was happy to have met Captain Cyprien Ngatoloéké and brought him to Lokossa.

By the time we had reached the town, it was already dark and I didn't fancy driving into an unfamiliar forest region, looking for a village I didn't know, at night. It made more sense to stop in town and proceed in the morning. The moment I mentioned this to the captain and asked where I might find a hotel, he insisted with a grin that I should stay with him. I would have to come to his house anyway, to collect his son as my guide. I didn't remember actually agreeing to take the lad, but since I hadn't definitely said "No," he assumed that his offer was accepted. I saw I needed to keep my wits about me.

His home turned out to be a scruffy little shed with concrete block walls and a tin roof, set inside a compound where three rectangular mud huts with thatched roofs jostled for space. The captain had a large family, with two wives and seven children ranging from nineteen down to two years old. There were a couple of other women there as well, but their role and status in the family wasn't explained. They might have been sisters or, more likely, mistresses – a common enough *ménage* in this region.

Something incongruous caught my eye immediately: a picture of the Madonna on the wall with a small votive flame burning beneath and a small dish of holy water in a bracket on the wall beside it. Facing it, on the opposite wall, were three large fetishes. One, an ugly carved mask daubed with yellow and white paint, had strings of shells, beads and seed pods festooned on it. Another was adorned with raffia, cowrie shells and feathers while the third looked remarkably like a shrunken human head.

I had never heard of such things being made in this country but, as this only a few dozen miles from the home of Voodoo, anything was possible. In the dim light of a paraffin lantern, it looked gruesome. All sorts of sinister interpretations leapt to mind and the prospect of sleeping on a bed directly beneath it was slightly daunting.

It had been a long day and I had been behind the wheel continuously for eighteen hours. Sleep came easily despite the unusual decorations above my head and I awoke having had no dreams I could recall. In the morning, when the light was better, I had a closer look at the third fetish and saw that it was a simian head, dried to look like it was human.

The captain's son was called Hernan. He was a bright lad, skinny as a racing snake, with a twitchy manner born out of his bubbling enthusiasm to be doing things rather than from any deficit. He was so keen to be helpful and his engaging manner was infectious. Fortunately he spoke reasonably good French, so we had no difficulty understanding one another. As we drove out of town, he began telling me lurid tales about the village we were going to, explaining that many of the people there held strange religious beliefs. He was a Catholic, he explained, but some of the villagers still believed strongly in spirits, fetishes and zombies while others were ardent Pentecostalists. It sounded an interesting mixture.

"If you and your family are all Catholic, what's that mask on your father's wall all about?" I asked.

"That is my other mother," he replied. "She is from a village near Dogbo-Itémé. It is her fetish."

So it was obviously acceptable to mix the two religions here, I concluded. That's tolerance. Perhaps it went further than that. In other parts of West Africa, I had seen how people in isolated communities could be good members of the congregation whenever the priest or missionary was around, but easily reverted to animist beliefs the minute his back was turned. They saw no problem in respecting both disciplines as, in their minds, neither was exclusive. I wasn't sure some of the missionaries would agree with this, but fortunately I didn't need to make any judgement about it. I have no problem with people holding different beliefs as long as they don't try to force theirs on me.

Listening to Hernan's chatter, I began to understand something of the beliefs held by the people I was about to meet. They lived in a forested part of the country, near one of the feeder streams of the Mono River. Wild oil palms spread along the slopes. The locals harvested the oil, selling some for cooking and using some to manufacture soap, which they sold in the markets of nearby villages and towns. He told me his aunt wanted to turn soap-making into a proper business and would no doubt ask for help with this. I asked if the soap was any good and he said I should judge for myself. It was what I had used this morning at his father's house. It had been good soap.

Like so many winding forest roads, this one suffered from lack of maintenance and the passage of many overloaded trucks, despite being close to several large towns. It took us two hours to reach Dogbo-Kotomé where we had to wait for a ferry to cross the river. The road on the other side was worse and our progress delayed by an overloaded lorry with a broken axle that was blocking the road to all but bicycles in both directions. It took an hour to cover the last seven miles to our final destination, Dogbo-Itémé.

Most of the village lay in a shallow valley where the original forest had been cleared. All that remained were a few giant trees, all over a hundred and fifty feet tall with huge root buttresses, scattered along the valley bottom among the houses. Looming over the settlement, they offered little shade but stood like lonely sentinels, a reminder of how the forest had been before man came with his chainsaw and felling axe.

The surrounding slopes were covered with a green patchwork of jungle and small cultivated fields. Secondary growth had filled the spaces at the edge of the forest when clearing the land had let light into the lower levels. The verdant growth sprawled across the land like a dense green carpet, speckled here and there with bright splashes of scarlet, yellow and purple where a tree was in gaudy bloom. From the centre of the village, the forest looked dark, forbidding and mysterious. As I discovered over the next few days, parts of it were. Few of the younger trees were more than fifty feet tall and none had such massive trunks as the giants in the centre of the village. Yet their variety was extraordinary and the number of orchids and other flowering parasites that lived in the canopy made it a botanist's paradise. As well as the plants, the range of birds, animals and insects inhabiting the forest was extensive, their calls, whistles, hoots and rasping adding a constant raucous background.

Our arrival soon attracted a crowd for, although the villagers were accustomed to passing motor traffic, not many strangers – let alone white men – stopped here, so I was an immediate object of curiosity. Hernan was obviously well-known and was soon slapping backs with friends and cousins.

The women who had asked me to call were away at the market in Dogbo-Kotomé and I realised that if we had stopped there a bit longer, we might have encountered them. But their family made us welcome and were soon plying us with a powerful forest brew they called *affal*. It was fruity and spicy and remarkably refreshing but needed to be treated with caution as it soon made my head feel slightly muzzy.

Before the liquor could have too much effect, Hernan insisted on taking me for a tour of the village. He realised that I was not used to this brew and knew that exercise would soon dispel its effects. It was also an opportunity for the rest of the curious villagers to have a look at me. Then, when it came to discussions with his aunts, they would give us space to talk. I wasn't sure the women were actually related to Hernan, but everyone older is either an aunt or an uncle among the forest folk, so I accepted their relationship.

The two aunts returned in a state of great excitement, praising God for their good fortune. Having successfully disposed of all the produce they had taken to the market, they brought back real money for some of their goods and useful items in exchange for the rest. They were delighted to hear that I had arrived to talk about their laundry project, and began praising God even more loudly for bringing me to them. The evening dissolved into a general celebration with frequent incantations in the form of impromptu prayers when people would stand up and do a little dance while offering up their praises.

It was an exciting and vibrant environment. This was going to be a very different visit from those I was accustomed to making among the more animist tribes. There would be no talking business today.

Christianity of a form I had not previously encountered, coupled with a real zest for life, was an intimate component of these people's lives. I realised my thinking would have to adapt to make sense of their ways.

Religious it might have been, but it was far from puritanical, and they threw a good party. After my initial encounter with the *affal*, I was careful what I drank that evening, not wanting a forest hangover to impair my faculties in the morning.

They were a most sociable and welcoming bunch but all through the evening I had that creepy feeling that someone was watching me intently. It was a crowded place, with people coming and going all the time and I was unable to identify who or where the watcher was. I tried my best to ignore it, but the feeling kept niggling at the edge of my consciousness.

DAWN CAME LATE AND slowly to Dogbo-Itémé. We awoke to a thin blue mist swirling through the tops of the sentinel trees, mixing with the straight rising columns of smoke from a few early cooking fires. It slowly dissipated as the sunlight strengthened, warming the upper levels of the air, and as an early morning breeze brought a little movement. It was after nine o'clock before sunlight fell upon the houses clustered in the valley bottom. By then, the temperature was starting to climb, the humidity was already over ninety per cent and the first trickles of perspiration were beginning to run down my back.

The moment I stepped outside I was aware of being watched. This time my observer was not so secretive. She stood directly in front of the doorway, twenty yards away, and made it plain she had been waiting for me. The woman didn't look very different from most of the others in the village, but there was no doubt that she was a witch. Her eyes gave her away; they had that piercing stare which sees far more than normal eyes. Lizard-like, they stared, unblinking, and I wondered if she was afraid of missing something if she blinked. This may have accounted for why the whites of her eyes were red and tired looking. She was concentrating hard on absorbing every scrap of information about me. It was a bit like being under the doctor's X-ray and slightly unnerving, for the woman was silent and unsmiling, offering no prayers or praise to the Lord like everyone else I had met.

At first I was inclined to ignore her but then decided to take the initiative. Walking straight up to her, I held out my hands and greeted her with the few words I had learned from my hosts the night before. A look of horror passed across her face before she turned and scuttled off screeching. This response wasn't what I expected. It left me standing there feeling like a fool for a few moments. Fortunately, not many people were about, so the incident didn't attract undue attention. I made my way across to where my hostesses were waiting for me.

"You've met our witch then," one of them announced.

"Yes. She was standing staring at me, so I thought it would be polite to say hello."

"Don't bother with that one," Asiakunu said. "She lives in another world. Few consult her but she is always there. She has turned her face from the Lord, but he does not want her spirit so she is still among us."

"She claims to speak with the spirits of the river," Djigénama added, "but we speak to the Lord."

The women told me they were sisters but they didn't look much like one another. Whenever one told me anything, the other always had to put a tail on it. This habit made discussions complicated as the tail often went in a different direction from the body of the conversation. Since the original speaker might then change tack, it took me some time to get used to their patter.

"Is she a priestess?" I asked.

"No, she has turned away from God and is mad," said Djigénama.

"But she makes fetishes and potions and, Lord preserve us, she also talks to the fish," Asiakunu added.

That was a new one on me. I understood sorcerers talking to the spirits, but not to fish. The strange woman was becoming more interesting by the minute.

I would have loved to have asked more, but I was here to discuss the laundry project and it was time to get down to business. It turned out that the two women already did laundry on a commercial basis but wanted to expand their operation to serve

*The original laundry pit. The river water was a
rich reddish brown, and silt-laden.*

clients from the nearby town. Their problem was that they used
river water for the laundry and this was far from clean. While
everybody used the same water, the amount of work involved in
getting laundry clean enough so they could charge money for doing
it was far more than anyone applied to their domestic washing.
What the sisters wanted to talk to me about was filtration, like I
had provided for the fishing villages around Lac Togo.

Together we walked down to the riverbank to inspect their
laundry facilities and to sample the water. The traditional washing
technique required the clothes to be soaked, then soaped and laid
on a smooth rock to be scrubbed. Once scrubbed, the garments

were rinsed and wrung out, being laid aside until a pile of washed items was assembled. The soaking pit, a depression in one of the rocks, was drained and refilled with 'clean' water from the river for rinsing. Some women merely rinsed their clothes in the current, but as the water was a rich reddish brown and carried a heavy load of silt, this didn't get them very clean and they had to be rinsed many times. By using a series of basins and bowls, some of the silt could be allowed to settle out before being decanted into the rinsing pit, thus reducing the number of times it had to be done. The final part of the process involved untwisting the wrung out garments, swinging them over the head and slapping them down hard numerous times on a clean, smooth rock to drive the remaining water out of the fabric. Garments were then spread over other flat rocks or hung on nearby bushes to dry in the sun.

We were nearly at the riverbank when the witch I had encountered earlier leapt out of the bushes in front of us. She must have been lying in wait for us. Chanting and flourishing the amulets that hung about her person on long cords of plaited palm leaf, she began gyrating and working herself into a frenzy. I asked the laundry ladies what was going on and they told me she was casting spells to protect the fishes. She said I was going to disturb them and because of this nobody would have any food. Her sister said the witch was calling a crocodile to come and eat me if I went in the water.

It didn't look like the sort of place crocodiles frequented and the current was quite strong, but I took note of the warning. I wasn't so sure about frightening the fishes and saw no sign that any of these villagers were active fishermen. Turning aside, we let the lady get on with her incantations and went to look at the laundry rocks.

That was the moment Djigénama exploded, calling on God to witness what a calamity had been wrought on her business. All three of the rock basins were filled with green slime. The surrounding rock was splattered with mud and twigs as if a load of earth had been dumped and then roughly scraped aside into the river. The cleft from which the women drew their water was filled with soil, topped with a pile of human excrement.

Djigénama 's explosion was nothing compared to the cold fury that Asiakunu displayed. She spun round, striding back to harangue the witch. She seized the wildly gyrating woman by the hair dragged her across the rocks. With a great heave, she hurled her into the nearest laundry basin, tripping her so that she landed head first in the green slime. A torrent of angry words, interspersed with loudly delivered prayers to the Almighty for retribution issued from both the laundry ladies.

A crowd soon gathered. In seconds, a ring of people, mainly women, surrounded the rocks, all adding their voices and calling out "Amen" to the prayers and adding to the angry cacophony.

I stepped backwards, not wanting to become embroiled in this fight, especially since at least one of the combatants was a witch who had already had a go at me. The press of bodies behind stopped me making a clean escape as they leaned forward to see what was going on. So I had to stand there among the yelling women and hope it died down quickly.

Djigénama was not going to let matters rest that easily. She found a stick and beat the witch while screaming wildly at her, calling on God to punish her. Every time the woman tried to crawl out of the slime-filled hole, one or other of the laundry ladies would push her back in.

This went on for a full ten minutes and I was beginning to

wonder how it would end when suddenly the energy subsided and here was quiet. The crowd to one side parted and a small man picked his way along the rocks, down to the riverbank. He looked like any of the village men I had seen the night before and I wondered if he might be the headman for the women to show him this much respect. Whoever he was, he commanded authority.

Despite the rest of the crowd having fallen silent, Djigénama and Asiakunu were still yelling at the woman when the man reached them. They were screaming that the Lord knew her sins in this matter and she should repent and do penance. She must pay for the loss of business this outrage had caused them. Without pausing for breath they turned to the man and, in only slightly moderated tones, carried on their torrent of words, pointing alternately to the woman, to the other washing basins and to the muck-filled cleft by the river. It took several minutes for their outrage to falter, but eventually they fell silent.

The man stood listening, not trying to interrupt or to ask questions, waiting until they were spent. By this time, the woman in the washing pit had managed to get herself the right way up and was scraping green slime off her face and head. She looked like a dreadful monster emerging from the swamp in a Grimm's fairy tale as she clambered unsteadily from the pit. The sides of the pit were too slippery with all the slime to make it easy for her to climb out and she had to crawl on her hands and knees.

When he spoke, the quiet man did not raise his voice enough for me to hear. Those closest to him listened attentively. Picking his way carefully over the rocks, he peered into each of the laundry pits and into the water-drawing cleft beside the river. Here he turned and beckoned the slime-coated witch, pointing down into the cleft.

He said something and she recoiled but he was too fast for her. His hand shot out, grasped her arm and pulled her back. As the green slime dripped from her onto the rocks, she slipped and fell, toppling over the edge into the cleft. The man said something else to her that the women standing nearest heard. There was a communal gasp and they began to whisper among themselves, turning away quickly to go about their own business as far away from the spot as possible.

HERNAN HAD BEEN noticeable by his absence this morning but he chose this moment to reappear beside me. I asked if he had seen what went on.

"No, but I heard it. The whole village heard it," he replied. "He has told the river witch to clean up the mess she has made or she will be seeing more of the fishes and crocodiles."

"Are there many crocodiles here?" I asked.

"I have never heard of one."

"What about fish?"

"The men of Dogbo-Kotomé are the fishermen. They catch big catfish and we trade for them."

"What do you trade?" I was interested in this barter economy in a region where the local economy appeared strong and money was commonly used.

"Fruit, palm oil, yams, charcoal, money, soap," he said. "All the normal things."

The laundry ladies decided to abandon the river for the day and retired to their compound to brew coffee and talk. Besides wanting to talk to me about their business, there was so much more to talk about after the morning's excitement. This would need to be gone over many times and every visitor to the compound would surely have something to say. It was certain that every woman who was on the riverbank that morning would visit the compound during the day to share her impressions and opinions about what had taken place. This was their way of dealing with situations like this.

As we walked back to the village I discovered other important things needed to be discussed as well. Asiakunu's family had received a marriage proposal for one of her four daughters. Tomorrow was the agreed day for the formal proposal to be presented. The marriage gifts were to be handed over and the bride given to her new husband. Under other circumstances, I might have described it as her wedding day, but it appeared they didn't do things quite that way here.

A wedding takes four days and involves palavers, feasting, prayers and a lot of dancing and partying. Rituals and formalities are taken seriously. Even though the girl would not be leaving the village and everybody knew all there was to be known about the parties involved, it was still important to do things right. That way, the ancestors and spirits would know what was happening and be suitably appeased.

This seemed incongruous, given the vigorously promoted Pentecostal Christian culture of most of the villagers. Everything they did was done in the name of the Lord. But they still considered it important to appease the ancestors.

When they told me about the wedding I offered to go away and come back at a more convenient time. Asiakunu and her sister wouldn't hear of it. Friends and relations were coming from villages all around and visitors brought good luck. Since I was visiting the bride's family, I must remain as part of their household.

When we reached the family compound, Asiakunu's husband,

Patrice, invited me to go and sit with the men. They would explain what was going to happen while we sampled beer that had been brewed for the festivities. This was an easy invitation to accept because I liked African village beer, having sampled many varieties across the continent.

It was clear that my original expectation of a relatively brief visit to assess this project had become unrealistic. Now I was sure to be here for an extended stay of a week or more. There only thing to do was relax and join in. So I went to drink beer and to get to know the men of the family. The work would get done in its own good time.

Hernan and I spent the rest of that morning with the growing gathering of men. The arrival of a new relative prompted another round of beer. Family news was exchanged with each newcomer and the Lord was praised for his bounty each time the jug was tilted. I was introduced to each new guest and had to explain many times what had brought me to the village. Although it wasn't needed because everyone understood the custom, Patrice explained to each newcomer why I had been brought into the family. Listening to the way he explained this, it slowly dawned on me that by ensnaring a stranger, the family had ensured the presence of an independent witness and arbiter if there should be any argument about the value of the marriage gifts. The significance of this only became apparent when it was too late for me to back out. I had drunk their beer and become an accepted part of the entourage.

During the course of the morning, the marriage customs of these people gradually unfolded. The union had been negotiated some time before when a woman approached Asiakunu on behalf of her son, asking if she would be willing for her daughter,

Akaniasa, to become his bride. At eighteen years old, the lad was well known to both Akaniasa and her mother – he lived only four hundred yards away on the other side of the village. This proposal had been long expected, but even so, the family still required a traditional sequence of extended negotiations to be fulfilled.

The bride's mother demanded to know how the proposed husband would care and provide for a wife, how he would treat her and what status she would have. That was important because many of the men had more than one wife. I never quite understood how that squared with their Pentecostal Christian beliefs.

In this case, it was academic. Kobiane was as yet unmarried, having been away from the village for a year training as a mechanic. Now he worked for the Highways Department at a depot about two miles north of the village, maintaining their road mending machinery. Established in a paid job, he was ready to marry his childhood sweetheart and start a family.

Ever since the day his mother had first approached Asiakunu about the marriage, he had spent his spare time building a new house at the back of Akaniasa's mother's compound. Because it was on the edge of the village, he first had to cut back the forest to make space. But this also provided building materials. He used the saplings he cut down to build a strong palisade around the plot. In this area of vigorous vegetative growth, it had been a major task. Many of the poles in the palisade had taken root, sprouted and were now growing bushy topknots of leaves. Thin side branches had been woven into the fabric of the fence, making it a strong barrier against intruding forest creatures or any domestic goats and fowls his future wife might choose to keep.

Akaniasa's new house was now completed and Kobiane was ready to claim his bride. Tomorrow, dressed in his finest new clothes, he would come and present his suit. Meanwhile, on the other side of the village, all his family were gathering, as Akaniasa's were here, bringing gifts for the marriage and joining in the celebrations. In brief moments of quiet, we could hear their voices, singing joyfully as family members arrived and offering up loud praises to God for bringing everyone safely to their compound.

By midday, I had drunk enough beer to keep me happy for a while and felt the need to be doing something active. I asked if it was permitted for me to view the new house Kobiane had built, but Patrice told me that would be part of tomorrow's ceremony. Today we must keep away and pretend the house was not there, even though it was less than twenty yards from where we sat.

15 ~ Scented soap

DURING A LULL WHEN several of our group wandered off to pay their respects and visit friends in the village, Hernan told me that soap was being made about a mile up-river. The relatives who were making it would certainly come tomorrow, but today they would be working. This was all the excuse I needed. I leapt at the chance to go and see how soap was made. Since we were going to visit family members, Patrice raised no objection. He thought it would be a good idea and quietly instructed Hernan to let the relatives know that I was the impartial family visitor.

We left before anyone else could object. I could see that Hernan too was keen get to get away from the slightly invasive formalities. As soon as we were out of the village we turned off the track, hurried into the forest and took a very long pee. The relief was exquisite.

"If you come here again in half an hour," Hernan told me as he emerged from a dense thicket, "there will be many little gold beetles where you pissed. They come to drink and are attracted by the ammonia. It makes them ready to lay their eggs."

Wonders would never cease; this scrap of information

fascinated me. It also impressed me that he knew so much about the forest and the insignificant creatures who lived in it. I grasped a bunch of leaves and bent them double, twisting a green twig round to make a marker so we could look at the beetles if we came back by this same path.

As we advanced, there was an increasingly pungent smell in the air, mingling with wood smoke. We turned off the main track and started downhill. It was obvious we were heading towards the river again. Before we got there, the trees opened out into a small clearing about fifty yards across. A dozen people were busy around three large steaming cauldrons and several long troughs.

Several women in brightly coloured clothes were stirring the cauldrons with long bent poles that let them stand several feet away from the heat while stirring. Two others were chopping wood to feed the fires while a third group was cracking the palm fruits and loading them into a fourth cauldron under which the fire had not yet been lit.

As soon as they saw us, those not tending cauldrons came over to greet us and give thanks to the Lord for bringing us to them. They all seemed very happy to see us, making our arrival feel like a special event. Hernan explained how I had come to see Asiakunu and Djigénama about their laundry business, and that I would be staying for the wedding. This brought more praises, a brief hymn and quick dance to celebrate the event. Their exuberance was infectious.

When they heard that I was interested in their soap making, they showed me around and explained the process. It all started with the palm oil fruits which had been brought from the forest in great bunches and left in a pile. The heap was over ten feet high. I thought it must have taken a tremendous amount of work to

Soap makers grind the palm oil kernels in a long wooden trough, ready to mix with saponin.

collect but they told me it was only a week's collection. The whole gang worked on a two-week cycle, collecting palm nuts one week and processing them the next.

The oil nut bunches had to be broken down and each nut bruised before it was put into the cauldron. This was hard work with a lump hammer and chisel to prise the individual fruits from the bunch. The fruits had an oily fibrous coating, so the first part of the processing was to bruise this and boil the fruits in water to release this oil. They skimmed off the oil for use in cooking and other domestic purposes.

When the fruits were cool enough to handle, they cracked and cooked them a second time to release the kernel oil. After this too had been skimmed off, the split husks were separated from the kernels which were like hard beans the size of a hazelnut. They spread these to cool on mats woven from palm fronds. When the kernels had cooled, they cracked them, scooped out the pulpy material inside and put it into a large trough made from a log. Using smooth, rounded stones from the river bed, they ground the pulp to a waxy paste against the side of the trough.

While this was going on, others were in the surrounding forest harvesting selected leaves which they crushed and stewed slowly over small charcoal fires. These leaves released saponin which is concentrated by the slow cooking. Mixed with the waxy paste, saponin gave the soap its cleaning properties. By the time they'd finished cooking these leaves, the brew smelled quite pungent and the soapiness was evident to the touch.

A number of aromatic herbs grew in the forest nearby. Some of these were collected to perfume the final product. By making strong infusions, their aromas can be captured and added to the final boiling, which was always done in a clay pot. I noticed that all the other cauldrons, in which the palm fruits were being boiled, were made of iron and asked why this final boiling had to be done in an earthenware pot. The answer was simple: the iron reacted with some of the perfume herbs and tainted the soap. If that happened, it couldn't be sold for a good price.

While the pulped kernels and the thick saponin syrup were being combined, I noticed a woman take three oranges and scratch the surface of each many times with a thorn before dropping the whole fruits into the cauldron. This, she told me, was to make orange-scented soap. The skin of the orange contained many tiny pouches of oil. "You can know this by squeezing the fruit. The oil comes out on your hands and smells sweet."

I stared at her. If there truly are Eureka moments, I was experiencing one of them.

I remembered the huge grove of bitter-tasting wild orange trees in south-west Mali. Here was a use for it, if only there was some way of collecting the oil. That started me wondering who else used orange oil, and used it on an industrial scale. It had to be the perfume industry. I made a mental note to enquire.

The scent of orange was strong during the final cooking and, as the sun disappeared behind the trees and the light began to fade, the woman in charge declared the cooking done. Tipping the cauldron carefully, they poured hot liquid soap into a series of moulds, carved into a huge hardwood log that had been split down its length. The moulds were inch-deep oval depressions about three inches long, gouged in serried ranks along the flat surface and polished smooth. Filled with hot liquid soap before sunset and left overnight to cool, they would yield a hundred bars of orange-scented soap the following morning, ready for sale.

As we thanked the soap makers and headed back to the village, I told Hernan we must come back in the morning and see the final part of the process. He laughed and said we would, if the Lord permitted it.

16 ~ A very joyful wedding

THE LIGHT WAS FADING BY the time we passed our bent leaf marker so it was too dark in the thicket to see any gold bugs. I felt disappointed. Never one to be discouraged, Hernan said we could look in the morning and, if necessary, pee again, then look on our way back. We would certainly have enough light then as we had to be back in the village before the end of the morning. The marriage petition was to be presented at noon. We were required to witness it and to join in the celebrations that followed.

Talking with Hernan about the convoluted marriage customs made me think again about the anomaly of the villagers being vigorous Pentecostalists and yet still adhering to many older, animist traditions. The formal petition for the marriage was to be presented in the form of a flat stone on which Kobiane's family had written all his virtues and the advantages he offered to the woman he wanted to marry. This included all the benefits her relations would accrue by bringing him into their family. Unlike most African societies where the bride, on her marriage, goes to live with her new husband's family, and is therefore lost to her own, here it was the other way round. The groom is adopted into the woman's family. They therefore needed to be convinced of the benefits of adopting him.

In Kobiane's case, as a salaried employee of a government department, the advantages were significant and obvious, but all his other attributes still had to be recorded and considered. Of course his family declared these qualities in the most glowing terms as part of their petition. They too had a stake in this affair; it was not simply an arrangement of promises between two individuals. Family benefits flowed in both directions, uniting them in many subtle ways. This process, involving everybody, ensured that things were well thought out beforehand and, not surprisingly, divorce was rare.

On receipt of the formal proposal stone, which was usually delivered by the groom's mother, the bride's parents held a brief conference before declaring their willingness to consider the rest of the petition. This was the last chance for anyone to raise objections to the marriage, the equivalent of a priest or registrar asking for anyone who knows of any reason why the couple may not be joined in matrimony to declare it.

Until now the process had involved only the women of both families, but now the men of the groom's family came forward to sing his praises, not forgetting of course to thank the Lord for making him such a virtuous man. Then the groom's family presented their wedding gifts in a theatrical stream. As we watched, each item was named and its quality and value proclaimed, accompanied by loud praises to the Lord for granting the givers such bounty. The purpose of this was to show that his family were people of quality who could be relied upon to help in times of dire need. Their support for the marriage demonstrated their acceptance of the bride's family and their willingness to be united with them. The gifts signified, among other things, their generosity of spirit towards their new in-laws.

Most of the marriage gifts were foodstuffs, but Hernan told me tools such as hoes and machetes might also be included, along with household objects: brightly coloured enamel bowls, cooking pots, knives and choice pieces of cloth. A complete outfit of clothing for the bride was always one of the gifts, as was a small amount of money, usually in silver coins. Maria Theresa dollars were popular because they were big and showy, but other silver coins from the colonial era were also commonly used.

The last thing to be handed over in this great offering was a large basket of yams. The size and quality of the yams was particularly important. Every adult female in the bride's family scrutinised each one before passing comment and praising the Lord loudly for having produced such beautiful yams and for guiding the hands of those who grew them. He also received praise for guiding those who chose the yams as part of the marriage gifts, and for endowing those who negotiated the marriage with such generosity and good judgement in their choice of the bride. He was truly a busy deity.

This ceremony took most of the afternoon and was lubricated with lots of beer and other forest beverages, but not food. That came later. Throughout there was singing and dancing; praises turned into hymns and everyone joined in. I didn't know the words to any of the hymns, but the people's evident joy as they sang, and their inviting hands drawing me into the dances soon made this unimportant. I was swept along on the tide of general merriment and celebration.

It was clear that this union was very popular. It united the whole community. Even the old witch, so reviled down by the riverbank the previous morning, was dancing and singing as though it was her own daughter being married.

It came as a bit of a shock after the yams had been presented to find myself at centre stage. I was sitting beside Akaniasa's father, watching a cluster of yams accumulating on the ground in front of me. There were seventeen yams in all, one for each year of the bride's life, and they were laid in a ring like a sunburst. When the last one had been placed in position, the groom's mother put a dish of cooked yams in the centre of the ring.

"Eat, and see that our yams are good," she said, handing me a wooden spoon and a small enamel bowl.

This took me completely by surprise. Nobody had warned me about this part of the ceremony. I looked at Patrice, sitting next to me, for guidance.

"Eat," he said, "and even if it is good, spit it out. Then take more from the other side of the dish and do the same. When you have eaten from all round the dish you can say the yams are good." He had a broad smile on his face as he told me this; clearly it was the opportunity for an element of fun and drama.

I took a spoonful of yam and dropped it in the small bowl. I scooped up a small amount with my fingers, rolled it into a ball and popped in my mouth. It was remarkably tasty – I would have liked to swallow it – but made a show of chewing for a moment and then spat it out onto a banana leaf by my feet. I turned the little bowl over and tipped out the remaining yam with a gesture of disdain before taking another spoonful from the other side of the main dish and going through the charade a second time. There was much sucking in of air as I took each mouthful, nervous anticipation from the watching families as I chewed, and a long sigh as I spat out each mouthful and tipped the small dish over.

After four mouthfuls, I leaned forward and examined the dish in the middle carefully. An expectant hush descended. Everyone else leaned forward as well, not wanting to miss anything. After a brief consideration I reached out and dug a portion from the centre of the dish, dropped it in the little bowl and sat back. Everyone else relaxed.

Slowly dipping my fingers into the mashed paste, I rolled some into a ball, put it in my mouth and closed my eyes. I wasn't sure how I was supposed to give my verdict on the yams. As nobody had told me about the convention beforehand, I had to wing it.

After a few moments gentle mastication I swallowed the mouthful I was chewing and took another. The families waited. I swallowed again and took another mouthful. After the third, the groom's mother asked anxiously, "Does he approve our yams?"

A wag at the back of the crowd called out. "Of course he does. He wouldn't continue eating if they were unacceptable!"

This, and my smile, provoked a squeal of delight from the groom's mother followed by a fresh outpouring of thanks to the Lord for guiding my choice and giving me such good judgement; for making the yams of superior quality and for anything else that happened to strike her at the time. The singing and dancing that followed went on for a full ten minutes.

The appearance of the village witch-doctor brought it to a halt. For a witch-doctor, he was dressed rather strangely. He had on a pair of blue jeans, slightly too short for him, a baggy red shirt and pink plastic sandals. Even so, there was no mistaking who he was: the bone ring through the septum of his broad brown nose, a host of dramatic whisker-like facial scars, the amulets that bedecked him and the iron objects hanging from cords over his shoulders and round his neck could belong to nobody else. He also had a long curving scar on his arm, almost half an inch wide, which looked as if the skin had been peeled off.

I had seen a scar similar to this on another arm some time recently. It wound around the arm from his left shoulder to his wrist in a spiral. It had the appearance of a snake, with his hand as the head and fingers and thumb being the opening jaws. I knew tattoos like this existed among other tribes, but I had never seen one in the form of a wide flat scar. The serpent obviously had a significance that was widely spread through different cultures.

This witch-doctor's hair was prolific compared with most of the men in the village, who kept theirs short. He wore his like a frizzy crown with assorted twigs and small feathers tangled in it. It looked in need of a good wash. He also had a small red feather thrust through a piercing in his right ear lobe.

Apart from these features, he looked like any other man in the village, with strong arms and callused hands, showing he was accustomed to hard work.

In the silence, the man stepped into the open space in front of me and reached down for the dish containing the remains of the cooked yam. He took a handful and smeared a little on each of the other yams laid in the ring around the dish. Taking another portion, he rolled it into a ball and put it in his mouth. With a little shuffling dance he made a circle round the display of yams and began chanting as he chewed. Eventually he had swallowed and his words became more distinct, but even Patrice, who was one of the older men present, said he didn't understand them. These were words for the spirits. He explained that the sorcerer was telling the forest spirits the yams offered for this marriage were good, and he was asking them to guard those who gave them and those to whom they were given.

AFTER ALL THE CHRISTIAN praises that had gone before, this was incongruous to me. Christianity may have taken root but it obviously hadn't displaced all the traditional beliefs in this forest community. The two belief systems lived in symbiosis, with no conflict between them. Nobody looked uncomfortable at the witch-doctor's involvement and when he finished there were loud cries of "Amen" and praises to the Lord for helping this man keep the forest spirits happy.

But there was more. Shortly after the witch-doctor had performed his rite and gone to sit and drink beer with the other village men, a pastor arrived, complete with clerical collar. He walked around and greeted all the men, including the witch-doctor, with a handshake and a few words, ending up beside Kobiane.

When the pastor had greeted everyone he began his part of the ceremony with prayers, loudly declaimed and energetically responded to by the assembled congregation with loud cries of "Amen". He led the singing of several hymns, accompanied by a pair of drums which appeared at the right moment from nowhere.

After working hard for nearly an hour, the pastor paused to drink some beer. When we had all refreshed ourselves and the Lord had been duly thanked for his bounty, the pastor resumed. Kobiane, led by two of his brothers, came forward to stand in front of the pastor who administered a lengthy catechism. He lectured him on all the responsibilities of marriage, asking him to confirm that he was willing to accept and discharge each one. He was, and each time he said so the congregation gave thanks.

Dusk was upon us before the pastor had finished and declared Kobiane fit to marry. Then it was the turn of the bride. There were loud protests from her family. Nobody was allowed to see the bride until she was married. The argument flowed back and forth for several minutes and as I was beginning to wonder what the problem was, Patrice leaned over and told me this was a normal part of the ritual. The bride would shortly be brought out, concealed under a red cloth, and the priest would question her like that. Her identity would be challenged by Kobiane as nobody but her female relatives had seen her face and it could be anyone under the cloth. "It's all a game," he told me.

And so it was. After ten minutes of ritual argument, Akaniasa emerged, hidden under a full-length red sheet. On either side, holding her arms, were Asiakunu and Djigénama. They steered her though the throng until she was standing in front of the pastor. The pastor's lecture and catechism was much shorter this time, but every response still elicited loud and enthusiastic praises from everyone watching. Not wanting to be left out, I too joined in, which seemed to please my hosts.

Singing and dancing erupted when the catechism ended and the pastor declared Akaniasa ready to be married. Even the bride did a little jig under her red shroud. The singing continued until a shrill female voice shouted out that it was not Akaniasa under the cloth. Kobiane stepped forward and demanded to see the bride's face. This might not be the right girl and it would be wrong for the family to foist an ugly sibling on him in order to get her married off. Proof was demanded.

This provoked loud protests from the bride's family and Patrice eventually stood up and calmed the crowd. It seemed there was a well-rehearsed ritual even to this as the crowd took several minutes to quieten down. Eventually Patrice asked the bride to give him her hands and one at a time they appeared from under the red cloth. He looked at the hands and announced to the crowd that these were the hands of his daughter Akaniasa and the right girl had made the promises. His declaration was dramatic and full of power.

As he looked round the throng, awaiting a challenge, a third hand emerged from under the red cloth, followed by a fourth. For a moment nobody noticed; everyone was still looking at Patrice. But then a giggle from under the red sheet drew people's attention back to the shrouded figure.

Pandemonium! The red cloth began to shake; the giggling underneath got louder. Suddenly the hem lifted and a small child burst out, running off to disappear into the hut behind us as the whole assembly erupted into peals of laughter. Patrice turned round, patted the shrouded figure all over to ascertain that there was only one girl under the cloth, and sat down.

Another hymn started and everyone joined in. The jubilation continued for about ten minutes. I was wondering when it would end, when once again everything stopped abruptly. There was total silence from the assembled revellers. Only the chattering of a small troop of monkeys in the forest behind us and the ringing call of an unseen bell bird somewhere in the forest disturbed the calm. But there was tension in the air and we all felt it.

These people certainly knew how to stage theatrical performances, I thought. I had no idea what to expect next, so I was unprepared for the dramatic return of the witch-doctor. Festooned this time with an antelope skin cloak, anklets of bells made from old food tins and little jingling brass bells at his wrists, Akgbegeyan erupted into the space vacated by the pastor, chanting and dancing around the betrothed couple as they stood facing one another. Now he wore a belt of monkey tails which swung out like a rising tutu as he spun on the spot, his voice rising to a crescendo. As he circled the couple, people in the audience began to sway,

The villagers were as exuberant in their dancing as in their praises to the Lord when celebrating the wedding.

starting a slow chant which everyone gradually took up. It started among the men, a deep rumbling sound, barely audible at first, but swelling as more and more voices joined in. To begin with it sounded almost menacing and I felt the hairs on the back of my neck rise. As the volume increased and lighter voices joined in, the tone lifted and it became something joyous yet enquiring.

A drum began throbbing in the background. The chant became more rhythmic, surging in volume as the pitch rose. At an unseen signal, it all stopped and the witch-doctor froze like a statue. After a moment, his posture relaxed and he walked towards the young couple, grasped the red cloth and with a flick of his wrist, whisked it off the bride, revealing her to the village.

A great sight, emitted by every throat there, confirmed the communal relief that this was indeed Akaniasa, and expressed their admiration of her beauty. She was indeed a very pretty girl, beautifully dressed in green and yellow clothes, her hair uncovered and braided into an intricate assembly of tiny plaits which formed a crown like a beehive on top of her head. This was the last time she would have her hair uncovered as women here always wore a turban of brightly coloured cloth once they were married.

I was still puzzled about what was going on when Hernan came and sat just behind me, leaning forward to whisper in my ear and explain the proceedings. Akgbegeyan's dance was to drive out evil spirits that might have been lurking, waiting to attack the bride and groom at the moment of their marriage. As he was the village's intermediary with the spirit world, it was his job to pacify them and to drive away any that were hostile. When I asked if this wasn't a bit of a contradiction to the professed Christian beliefs, he was askance at the suggestion.

"Not at all," he said. "God has nothing to do with the forest spirits. They have always been there. They were there before God came to us. We can't ignore them. Akgbegeyan looks after the spirits and Pastor Gabriel looks after *le Bon Dieu*."

His attitude needed a bit of digestion and I'm not sure I ever understood it fully. But all the people I talked to over the next few days found it a perfectly normal and acceptable approach. It suited their lives admirably. When they had concerns that were the affairs of God, they prayed vigorously, with absolute belief in God's goodness and salvation, and consulted the pastor. What he taught them was about their souls and they invested heavily in protecting them in the present and for the future. Anything to do with spirits or malevolent influences was the realm of the fetish priest, and he was Akgbegeyan. So he still had an important role in village life.

"You can see more of this if you go to Abomey," Hernan told me. "There is the home of Voodoo. Those people also recognise

God, but for them the spirits are much more important and they esteem those who have died but are not dead. For us, they are nothing."

"Do you mean zombies?" I asked.

"They are abominations of the Devil." Hernan was vehement. "They have no place here."

I already knew a little about Voodoo and was aware that Abomey was the centre from which it sprang. From there the Voodoo cult had been exported to the Caribbean by the slave trade. The town was only a few miles north-east of this village, but Dogbo-Itémé was a bit of an enclave of Christianity because a medical missionary had come here about thirty years earlier, when there had been a plague outbreak. His work had left a lasting legacy among the people. He treated the sick and shared his Pentecostal beliefs with them. They in turn decided that his God was responsible for the miraculous success of his treatments. Although I found nobody who had actually met this missionary, from the way everyone spoke about him, he must have been a remarkably charismatic and joyful man, as well as a good doctor. His manner was so infectious that people willingly adopted his beliefs. They told me very proudly that there had not been a serious outbreak of illness in the area since those days, thanks be to God. Such illness as occurred was always relatively minor and easy to attribute to malevolent spirits. These, everyone knew, were always hanging around looking for victims and opportunities to cause trouble. It sounded as if these people shared many of the beliefs of the Calabar tribes from further east in the Niger delta.

AFTER THE DRAMATIC revealing of the bride, the ceremonies paused while the villagers refreshed themselves with more beer, ignoring Kobiane and Akaniasa who were able to exchange a few words. Up to this point the couple had not been allowed to touch one another. Now, as the ceremonies resumed, the witch-doctor produced a bowl of evil-smelling liquid and made each dip their hand in it. He then emptied the bowl into a hole in the ground. With a bowl of water and a cake of the soap from that morning's batch, Akgbegeyan washed the hands of the bride and groom, purifying them for their union and ensuring that, as all the dirt or evil spirits had been washed from them, there was nothing to come between them in their marriage.

They were now ready to be married: re-enter Pastor Gabriel. In a few brief sentences, he asked Kobiane and Akaniasa for their consent to the marriage and gave long-winded thanks to the Lord for having brought them successfully to this point. "Amen!" the assembled families added enthusiastically. The pastor blessed them as a married couple, the deed was done and the partying began in earnest. The two families merging to talk and dance together, friends seeking each other out, children playing. The symbolism was heavy and, as the two groups mingled, friendships that were already well established were further strengthened.

THE SINGING, DANCING AND feasting carried on long after I was collapsing with weariness. When I eventually crawled off to the hut where I had slept the night before, I found several people already sleeping there. I joined them on the communal grass mattress and was asleep in moments.

Wakefulness came suddenly in the morning when someone inadvertently stepped on my foot and offered profuse apologies. It was late. The sun was already bright in the courtyard outside as I hastily dressed and went out to see what was going on.

What was going on was more of the same. Apart from the sunshine, the scene had hardly changed from that which I had abandoned in favour of sleep. Many members of the two families were still singing, dancing and passing food around. When they party, these people really party!

As I listened, I identified hymns with liberal sprinklings of hallelujahs and similar religious elements. Others sounded like traditional songs, similar to those the women had been singing when I visited the soap-makers the previous day. They reminded me of *puirt a beul* in Scotland, where the songs give momentum to the work and make tedious tasks feel less onerous by sustaining the working rhythm. This morning, three drummers provided a continuous rhythm and a man with a balafon played melodies to which a few people were adding their voices.

I looked around for anyone I had been speaking to the night before. I eventually found Patrice, huddled in a corner with two old men. He looked uncomfortable, as though they were berating him over something. The moment he saw me, his face brightened and he gestured to call me over. He rose to greet me like a long-lost brother. Muttering something to his two companions, he took my elbow and led me away saying loudly: "You have come just in time, there is something I have to show you."

"What is it?" I asked.

"Nothing," he said when we were out of the others' earshot. "I needed to get away from those two boring old men. They're trying to drag me into something I don't want to do. You rescued me. Let's go into the forest."

So we went into the forest. After a few minutes, we found a cluster of wild banana trees. Several bore fruit which was beginning to ripen. Patrice drew his knife and cut off a few ripe bananas and we sat on the ground eating them while he explained about the scheme the others had been trying to involve him in. It didn't make much sense to me but it was obviously a relief for him to be able to talk freely and get it off his chest.

We finished our fruit and continued further into the forest, describing a wide loop that would bring us to the riverbank near the soap-makers. As we walked, the undergrowth thinned and we came to a fetish tree in a small clearing. This lone tree towered high above the surrounding forest, looking both statuesque and sinister because above head height the trunk and branches were unnaturally black.

The forest hereabouts was all secondary growth, with very few great trees remaining. Most of the canopy was only thirty or forty feet above ground, so this big kapok tree, which must have been over a hundred feet tall, really looked like a giant. It had huge buttressed roots and a tall straight trunk covered in heavy thorns. The lowest branches were far above the general canopy height. A host of fetish gifts had been placed around its base. Some of these were crude carvings, representational figures; others were votive items like seeds, fruit husks, shells and brightly coloured bits of plastic or glass beads. Some of the offerings were composite items made with feathers, leaves and sticky resins. Others were composed of bits of animal skins, bones and strangely shaped pieces of pottery. In places the altar had been dusted with flour or red powder and there was at least one small calabash containing congealed blood.

It was a malodorous place with a sinister atmosphere. I had the impression something was missing but could not put a finger on what it was. Only as we were leaving did I realise that the surrounding forest was silent and there were no flies. Usually

Offerings left underneath the fetish tree... a malodorous place with a sinister atmosphere.

exposed organic matter or food left out in the open anywhere in the tropics will attract flies. More often than not, the worse something smells, the more flies it attracts and you hear a continual background buzz of tiny wings. The absence of flies and buzzing around the base of this bizarre tree was eerie.

Turning away, I saw Patrice remove something from his pocket and drop it at the foot of the tree.

"Should I leave an offering?" I asked him, not sure of the significance of this particular shrine and what etiquette demanded.

"No," he said. "I have asked the spirits to make those men leave me out of their schemes. You only leave something if you have a request to make."

"Do the spirits see beyond this bit of forest here?"

"They are spirits, how can we know what they see?" Patrice sounded confused by my question. "If you have a request, leave something beside the tree and ask the spirits. If they accept your gift they may help you, or" – he laughed a little nervously – "they may ignore you. It is not for us to know the mind of the spirits."

Like insurance companies, I thought, the spirits always have an infallible get-out clause.

As we left the fetish tree, I saw something moving across the path which attracted my interest. It was brown and scaly and I thought I recognised it. Rushing forward, I reached between the bushes as it was about to disappear and grabbed, coming up with a wriggling monster in my hand. The tail which I had grabbed wrapped firmly around my wrist and the animal tried to turn back on itself, its claws scrabbling to climb my arm.

Patrice was horrified and recoiled, stepping back to be well clear of it and me. "Put it down! Let go of it!" he shouted.

"Why? It's only a pangolin," I protested.

But Patrice was having none of it. "No, it's Simelenkele," he said in awed tones. "He is the worst of the forest gods and can cause you great trouble. You must let him go and apologise."

Having caught the scaly beast, I wasn't about to let it go. I had never handled one before and wanted to have a good look at it before letting it return to the forest. I knew people elsewhere would want to eat it but here they appeared to have other ideas about these scaly ant-eaters.

Patrice was most unhappy about my wanting to hang onto the animal and inspect it and even more reluctant when I wanted to take it back to the village.

"It can only bring bad luck," he insisted. "You must not offend Simelenkele. He will bring misfortune to the village."

"We'll take him back and consult the fetish priest, then."

"He will curse you for it," Patrice said, keeping his distance.

Since I was nearer to the track back to the village, I turned and started walking. "I'll let the animal go after we've had a look at it and shown Akgbegeyan," I said over my shoulder.

With great reluctance Patrice followed, ten paces behind, muttering to himself. The pangolin, meanwhile, had curled itself into a ball and was no longer trying to escape. I was able to have a good look at its scaly back and small curved claws as I walked.

When we got back to the village the fetish priest was nowhere to be found, but I soon had a crowd of excited children all wanting to look at my captive. Curiosity rather than fear was their forte and it didn't take long for a small brown hand to reach out and touch the scales. Soon they all wanted to stroke it. The pangolin remained tightly curled, its head buried inside its coiled body. It was a wonder it could breathe like that, with its nose hidden.

We had been back in the village only a few minutes when the witch who had accosted me the first morning and caused all the trouble at the laundry site arrived brandishing a stick. She was yelling and swearing, apparently telling me I had no right interfering with the gods and making them prisoner. The children laughed at her.

As she tried to hit me with her stick, I snatched it from her hand. Her shrieking attracted others and a crowd soon grew. Patrice, meanwhile, had managed to find Akgbegeyan who pushed his way through the press of bodies to see what all the noise was about.

He peered at the animal and asked me to hold it up by the tail. As soon as I did so, it reached out a claw and grasped the stick I had taken from the witch. In seconds it was trying to climb this, its tail now wrapped firmly round the stick. Like this it was easier to see and everyone could get a good look at its small snout, beady

The Tree Pangolin, Manis tricuspis. Some of the
villagers feared it was the wicked god Simelenkele.

eyes and long scaly form. It was sandy brown and looked like a
streamlined dragon from a fairly tale.

I heard Patrice still going on about it being Simelenkele and
asked the witch-doctor if this was so.

"He can take this form," he replied, "but he would never let
you capture him. This is not Simelenkele or you are his man and
he is your friend. I will make a divination."

This sounded a bit ominous. I wasn't sure I wanted to be
identified as the agent of a god people obviously feared. At the
same time, I knew this animal was harmless and the children
obviously had no fear of it. At least nobody had suggested it
should be killed and eaten. It was probably its identification with

Simelenkele that prevented this. Nobody wanted to offer the nasty god that sort of insult, even if they didn't entirely believe in him.

The witch doctor went off to do his divination and the children came forward to take turns holding the pangolin, turning the stick up the other way to make it climb. Its climbing ability clearly identified the animal as a tree pangolin. I hoped it wouldn't be upset by the children's handling as this species was known to excrete a noxious-smelling substance from their anal glands when upset or threatened. That would undoubtedly conform Patrice's assertion that this was Simelenkele and anything I hoped to achieve with these villagers would be severely prejudiced.

So after we had all had a good look at it, the pangolin had to be returned to the wild. I asked the children if they knew of a big ants' nest in the surrounding forest. They did, so we all trooped off in its direction.

Before we found the ants' nest, the witch-doctor caught up with us. He wanted to see how the animal behaved in the presence of the ants. He watched with interest as I uncoiled the animal from the stick, rolled it into a ball and trundled it onto the seething ant heap. It was covered in ants in seconds but rapidly uncoiled and begun feasting itself on its attackers. They weren't able to penetrate its scales so their attack was ineffective and the animal immediately released its noxious smell, repelling most of the ants. We could smell it from fifteen feet away and it really was foul, worse than any skunk. I could now understand why some people associated this inoffensive animal with the odious Simelenkele.

"So," I asked the witch-doctor, "is that the god or an animal?"

"Simelenkele is many things," he said enigmatically and walked off without a backward glance.

WHEN WE RETURNED to the village, Asiakunu was looking for us. She wanted to introduce me to the other members of her family involved with her laundry business and saw no reason why the celebration which had brought them all together should not be exploited to get decisions made. She had rounded up eleven people who were crucial to the operation. Some of them lived in nearby towns and would be employed collecting the dirty washing and returning clean items to their owners. Others would be doing the laundry: washing, rinsing, drying, folding and ironing the garments. Her youngest son, who was doing well in school, was to be the record keeper. Another of her sons, Folomé, had a little mechanical expertise and was taking on responsibility for the water supply. It was with him that most of my involvement would be. The business was investing in a pump which he would operate and maintain, so this made sense.

Asiakunu and Djigénama said they had heard about me from a relative married to a Togolese man. She had told them about work I had done across the border providing filtered water to people in the fishing villages around Lac Togo. So they had invited me here in the hope I could help them with similar filters.

In Togo, we had used a sub-sand abstraction filter which worked on the principle of a biological mat. For this, the sand served only as a conduit for the water to flow though. When water was drawn down through sand to a collection box, organic matter collected on the sand's surface forming a mat that acted as a biological filter. The mat was held in place by the suction through the sand. If it became too clogged to permit the passage of water, the suction would decrease, allowing the mat to float off. With the suction now restored organic matter would again collect and form a new filter mat. In this way it acted as a self-cleaning filter, needing

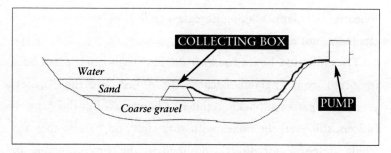

Basic structure of a pumped sub-sand abstraction filter.

little maintenance and with no moving or replaceable parts. Provided a reliable pump was available, it was ideal for bush use.

The original idea for this filter came from George Cansdale, the celebrated zoologist, who had spent some years as a forestry officer in Ghana. During his later career, he ran a marine zoo in England where he started using sub-sand abstraction to provide clean seawater for his specimens. Remembering the need for clean water in Africa, and always willing to share ideas freely, he generously taught me about the technique, first demonstrating it in a muddy pond outside his house. He continued to offer helpful advice and ideas when I began applying the principle in the West African bush.

The filter requires a fibreglass box of about eighteen inches cubed, open at the bottom and with a slotted screen inside it. This collection box is placed over and covered with large clean stones, before being buried in sand, open side downwards. The sand covering needs to be at least six inches over the top of the box. Through a nozzle attached to the top of the box, water is drawn along a pipe by a surface-mounted suction pump.

In the early 1970s, modern plastics were just beginning to be used in Africa. While their use was not something within the usual cultural orbit of African artisans, I was confident in their ability to learn and adapt. Making fibreglass collection boxes was only a challenge, not a problem.

The collection boxes used on the Lac Togo project had been imported from England. Because the project had the Togolese President's personal backing, this had been easy. But the customs officers still eyed the boxes with suspicion and I knew that any similar imports not directly destined to this project would be subject to demands for high duty payments, interminable paperwork and long delays. It was therefore important to find a local source or someone who could make them.

It was fortuitous to find a local car mechanic right here in Dogbo-Itémé village who, once he saw fibreglass being laid down, soon understood its potential for mending car bodies. It was only a small step from mending car bodies to producing filter boxes.

The mechanic's name was Djegbo and he embraced the new technology with great gusto. It didn't take him long to make four boxes to the specification I required for the laundry project. Over the next three years, he supplied many others which went into filters all over West Africa, even as far away as northern Senegal. His car repair business flourished too and within a few years he had branched out to make decorative attachments, like aerofoils, spoilers and air intake scoops.

Djegbo never let me down when I wanted either a single or a dozen filter boxes for a new project, even at short notice. That was his way of thanking me for opening a new door for his business by introducing him to fibreglass.

The only difficulty in the early days was ensuring that he had enough materials. With nobody producing resin and glass fibre matting in Dahomey, they had to be imported, but the commercial agents were ready and willing to arrange supplies. This being

Dahomey, not Togo, the customs officials were a little less stringent and devious; not so greedy for bribes. I had also made a friend of Captain Cyprien Ngatoloéké when I arrived and favours can work both ways.

ASIAKUNU'S SON FOLOMÉ, a thick-set chap of about twenty-five, had a better than basic understanding of things mechanical, but no formal training. Since he would have to look after and operate the pump, this was important. I arranged for him to get a few hours of instruction from the men in the servicing department of the John Holt Company, who were supplying the pump.

Once they had shown him how the pump worked, he was quick to understand. He pointed out that drawing water from the cleft that was currently used might pose problems as there was a strong eddy which would soon scour away the sand layer. This demonstrated his understanding in exemplary fashion. Retention of the sand layer was vital to the success of the filter and while the technique had been used in rivers before, none flowed as fast as the stream here.

After a bit of thought, Folomé asked if the source had to be immediately adjacent to the washing area. There was a pool upstream, near the soap makers, that was still. We went to look and found a round pool dug into the river bank where clay had once been removed for building materials and for making pots. It was nearly forty feet across and, when we waded in, over five feet deep. A large quantity of vegetable matter brought down by the current had accumulated where the pool joined the river. Some of this was embedded in the bottom and there was a layer of debris floating on the surface. The pool needed a little bit of cleaning out, but to add to its advantages there was a broad track down to the pool, worn by countless feet when it had been used as a clay pit. This would allow us to deliver loads of stone and sand for making the filter bed.

We spent half an hour discussing what needed to be done before going back to the village to plan a water system for the laundry. Besides the cleaned-out pool, it required a delivery pipe, a storage tank at the washing area and a bigger pump than I originally intended, as it would have to pump the water nearly half a mile to the laundry site. The laundry ladies were willing to invest in this venture and didn't see the increased cost of the pump as a problem. What they mostly needed from me was help with cleaning the water.

Others joined in while we were discussing how to develop the pool and ideas started to flow. Before long, this had become a community project. The whole village stood to gain from having a clean water supply, so offers of labour and materials were soon forthcoming from all sorts of different people. By mid-afternoon, it looked as if we were planning a new water supply for the entire village, which at that time numbered about six hundred and fifty people.

I didn't mind. This made much better use of my expertise and resources and, since the whole community was going to contribute, it was more effective development and time well spent.

OUR DISCUSSIONS HAD TO wait when further wedding celebrations took over the latter part of the day. It was time for the new bride and groom to be installed in their new home. This was the hut built specially for them adjacent to Asiakunu's hut, inside the stockade Kobiane had constructed.

For this part of the proceedings, the witch-doctor again had a central role, driving out loitering evil spirits and daubing the hut with protective powders and potions. He hung herbs and amulets in the rafters and poked a protective charm into the thatch to deter the spirits known to have a propensity for setting fire to roofs. Before he was done, he had danced and waddled his way round the building five or six times, chanting sacred spells. For the last of these circuits, he took the newlyweds by the hand and then led them inside. The three of them remained inside for a full twenty minutes. The rest of us stood around waiting and chatting.

Eventually Akgbegeyan emerged, pulling the door shut behind him and without a word walked off, disappearing in the throng. Hernan was standing near to me and I asked what all that had been about.

"It is to seal the marriage," he explained. "Akgbegeyan has driven out the evils spirits and purified the house. Then he had to remain and see that the marriage was consummated."

"You mean he had to watch them having sex?" I asked.

"Of course! Is there any other way to consummate a marriage?" The idea seemed a little odd to my Western mind, but the African part of me understood it was quite normal. Life here was raw and uninhibited, yet there are taboos, just as in any society. Having evolved over thousands of years, and being mostly rooted in the spirit world, their approach fitted the culture and the people well.

Gourds of beer began circulating after the witch-doctor had gone and the celebration became a joyful party. The drummers began to play and before you could blink, there was a circle of women shuffling, stamping and swaying. Men formed another ring, dancing outside the women's circle and moving in the opposite direction. Hands reached out, pulling me into the circle.

Draining my beer bowl and passing it to one of the women waiting to fill it for someone else, I joined the dancing line.

As my feet sought the shuffling step, my mind was trying to figure out how many gallons of beer had been drunk over the last few days. It must have been many hundreds, and all brewed here in the village. It wasn't only beer we had drunk; a variety of other concoctions had been passed around at special moments during the ceremonies as well. They were a boozy lot, these villagers, and yet I had not seen anyone seriously drunk.

17 ~ One of the family

LATER THAT EVENING Folomé touched me on the arm and drew me aside. He wanted to tell me about a quarry used by the government road menders. They had stocks of gravel and sand and he wanted me to drive him over there in the morning to see if we could get the materials required for the filter. This sounded like an ideal solution as it would be far quicker than collecting the materials in small baskets and carrying them to the pool on heads. Folomé had already organised a gang to start clearing the accumulated trash from the pool, so this visit would make good use of my time in the village.

His sense of urgency and 'can do' attitude were impressive. Such behaviour was uncommon here. I normally found myself bogged down in lengthy negotiations to get the simplest tasks done, even on projects which the people desperately wanted to see carried out. Someone always had to argue the toss.

The government quarry was six miles from the village. It held huge stockpiles of materials which made it easy to identify what we needed. Acquiring any was more complicated. The quarry was run by a little man who was full of his own importance and immune to any form of inducement or persuasion. He required the proper documented authorisation before anything left his stockyard. Unfortunately he spoke no French, so I had to leave all the talking to Folomé and Hernan, who had also come along. After half an hour, the man reluctantly showed us examples of what documentation was required and told us where to get it. As he pointed out, it required at least three different signatures, two revenue stamps and a series of confirmatory rubber stamps to be properly authorised. I made the mistake of thinking we could just nip off to town to get these. This was hoping for too much. We had to get the form from one office, take it to another for verification and payment of the administrative fee and then go to a third office for approval and another rubber stamp.

Since the materials were not normally available except to government agencies, this meant they would have to be purchased. An additional special permit would be necessary for this. We had to obtain this permit and pay for the goods before the requisition form could be issued and processed. Obtaining the special permit should have required a visit to the local Préfecture and to the Caisse Nationale to make the payment and to get the right rubber stamps impressed on it, but the quarry manager told me somewhat gleefully that the system had recently been changed. Now only an office at the Ministry of the Interior in the capital issued the form – and it had to be taken back to the same office to be stamped after the payment had been made and a receipt issued by the local Caisse.

He was joking, of course? The look on his face told me he wasn't. He was very much a 'job's worth' man.

I asked if he could show me an example of this special form to ensure that I obtained the right thing. He said he didn't have one and had never actually seen one, but if I presented the form, correctly stamped, he would know it. Short of going to the capital and joining the merry-go-round of bureaucracy, there seemed little alternative.

Hernan suggested we should approach the Highways Department. Their maintenance depot was not far away. So we said goodbye to the quarry manager and drove along the road.

The manger at the depot was a most obliging fellow whose brother lived in Dogbo-Itémé. Over lunch at the nearby café, we explained our dilemma. He understood and without hesitation issued a document that would release five tonnes of medium grade stones and fifteen tonnes of fine sand. He offered the use of a Highways Department truck and driver to deliver it all to the village as well, and all this without the need for any payment or inducement. We agreed a delivery date for three days time and promised to make sure that the track was cleared sufficiently to get his truck all the way down to the river bank for a convenient drop off.

I felt really good; the project was coming together. A trip to a town where there were proper communications was now required to arrange for a filter collection box to be flown out from UK. We also needed to find and buy a suitable diesel-powered pump. The pump proved to be no problem and we loaded it into the back of my Land Rover at the John Holt's store. Getting the filter box would take a week but, as an alternative, I was offered a strong plastic drum; we could cut that down and attach a pipe using store-bought fittings. With a little tinkering, the bottom of the drum could be made to fit inside its middle. With slots cut in it and a ring of pop rivets to secure it in position, I thought this would serve quite well. A threaded plastic fitting fixed the take-off pipe to the thread that previously secured the drum's cap and it was ready to install. We bought 150 feet of two-inch reinforced flexible hose for the suction side and a further length to go between the pump and a storage tank.

IT WAS A MERRY BAND who drove back into the village that evening. We were in time for supper with the extended family. This was being doled out by Djigénama and two of her daughters. The family were seated all round the open space in the centre of the compound, so I found a vacant spot, next to an old man to whom I had not yet spoken, and accepted a bowl of soup and mashed yam.

The old man was Asiakunu's father and after a few moments I noticed he wasn't eating his food. His bowl of soup, with a spoon in it, sat ignored on the ground in front of him. I looked at him carefully to see if there was something wrong and realised his hands were so twisted with arthritis he was couldn't hold the spoon. He was waiting for one of his granddaughters to finish handing out food before she came to help him.

When I picked up his bowl, filled the spoon and offered it to him, he gave me a broad smile and a slight nod of thanks as he opened his mouth and accepted the food. I gave one spoonful to him followed by one for myself and we continued to eat together. After the third or fourth spoonful, I noticed that he had no yam in his bowl so I rolled a small portion from my own into a bite-sized piece and offered this. An immediate twinkle appeared in the old man's rheumy eyes. He proceeded to chomp with toothless gums, savouring it with sublime pleasure.

We had been eating together for several minutes when Djigénama came over to attend to the old man. "Well Kebu," she said, "have you found someone new to feed you? I see you are eating all his yam."

The old man swallowed what he was eating and mumbled something. It barely sounded like words but was evidently intelligible to Djigénama for she burst out laughing. Rocking back with her hand on her broad hips, she hooted with delight. I looked at her quizzically, hoping for an explanation of the joke as she made a shuffling pirouette.

"Praise the Lord, I have a son," she announced loudly to the assembled family. "Kebu tells me he has a new grandson. He is adopting Ian who has shared his food with him."

There was general applause and a few more loud praises before a voice from the other side of the courtyard called out, asking if Djigénama wanted formally to adopt me; if so, I had to be initiated. This provoked a lot of excited conversation. Everyone had an opinion on the suggestion and it was impossible to keep track of who said what, so I just continued feeding the old man.

By this time I understood that the old man's name was Kebu. He spoke no French so we had no language in common, and he was indeed Djigénama and Asiakunu's father. He looked old enough, his face like a wrinkly brown walnut, but he still had plenty of life in him. He was clearly ready to express his opinions, even though in this largely matriarchal community he had no special status other than his advanced years.

Kebu's quiet manner and great age reminded me of Ayenu, the quiet man I had met in the stick hut far away in south-west Mali. I wondered how he and Nasia were getting on after returning from the dead.

By the time we finished eating, I realised that something out of the ordinary was happening. There was a more vibrant hum of conversation. People were gathering and kept looking in my direction. Hernan sidled over and told me that Djigénama had decided to adopt me; she had no sons since her only boy had died a couple of years earlier. A tree had fallen on him in the forest while he was cutting wood.

"Have you been circumcised?" he asked, as if this was a perfectly normal topic for discussion. Momentarily taken aback by his question, I told him it had been done when I was an infant and asked why he wanted to know.

"Because a man cannot be initiated unless he has been cut. Among our people we circumcise boys when they are twelve and they are initiated as men the following year. The women are arranging your initiation now so that Djigénama can adopt you."

"What does this mean?" I asked.

"Initiation lets the spirits see your soul so they will know you. There will be marks that let the people know you are a man who is part of this community. Then you can become part of the family." He grinned at me.

"Why does she want to adopt me?"

"Because her father told her she should. He said you would be a good grandson, better than his worthless granddaughters who deny him any yam," he replied. Seeing the incomprehension on my face, he continued: "The women never give him yam because it is too much work rolling it so he can eat. They just pour soup into him with a spoon. But you shared your yam. He likes yam. So he told his daughter to adopt you, hoping that you will do this again."

"I don't need to be adopted to do that," I laughed. "I would do it anyway if he likes it."

Hernan laughed at this and went on to explain some of what the initiation involved. It sounded slightly daunting and I felt a flutter of butterflies in my stomach. Or was it the food? We sat chatting for a few minutes, the old man occasionally patting my arm with his twisted hand and grinning happily whenever I looked at him. It was impossible not to return his smiles as he was obviously very happy with what was happening.

For a brief moment, I wondered what my own mother would have made of this turn of events. She would certainly have expected me to help him with his food; that was basic good manners. But I suspected she would be highly amused that Djigénama wanted to adopt me and possibly a little flattered. Although older than Djigénama, my mother had spent some years in Africa and many more in India, where she liked and got on well with the indigenous people. It was not simply my own disposition, but the many things she had taught me and her example of welcoming diverse strangers into our home that let me feel comfortable living and working among people like these.

THE FETISH PRIEST APPEARED with an armful of assorted items. He assembled a small table and covered it in strange objects. There were several small gourds, bunches of dried herbs, some fresh leaves and flowers, and pots that contained resinous goo which I could smell from twenty feet away. A hollowed log mortar, usually used for mashing yams and pounding grain, was placed upside down nearby to provide another flat surface.

I watched, fascinated, as Akgbegeyan began mumbling and mixing something in an empty calabash. I was so wrapped up in what he was doing that I almost missed hearing what Hernan whispered in my ear.

"He will purify you now. Then you will be washed and the spirits will be called to meet you."

Before I could reply, hands took mine and pulled me to my feet, leading me towards the upturned mortar. I was pushed down to sit on this and the hands released me. There wasn't even time to register whose hands they had been before the sorcerer was standing in front of me offering the small calabash. He told me to drink the contents and drain the bowl in one draught.

Wondering momentarily what I had got myself into, I took the calabash. In retrospect, it is impossible to explain why I didn't question anything, but I didn't. I just did as he instructed, and swallowed the liquid. At first there was no taste, but after a few seconds faint flavours began to dance around my tongue. In less than a minute, the inside of my mouth had become numb. My throat felt tight and then it too went numb. The sensation was spreading and by the time it reached my belly it felt like burning. It was too late now, but I wondered if I had swallowed acid. The effect didn't last. It soon passed, leaving me light-headed.

The sorcerer was skipping round me chanting mystical words. These must be the call to the spirits, I assumed, pleased that I still appeared to have control of my thoughts and reason. I was wondering how long this state would last when he went to his table and picked up a small flask that had been sitting there with a cloud of little flies buzzing around the twisted leaf stopper. Pushing my head back, he put the flask to my lips and poured in a few drops of the contents. It tasted absolutely diabolical. I wanted to spit it out but he stroked my throat and made me swallow. Before I could protest, it was gone and the intensity of its taste subsided.

Akgbegeyan resumed his dance, circling in the opposite direction. My senses began to feel fuzzy, my finger tips and toes tingled and I felt as if I was swaying on the stool. Hands took hold of my arms, and a few moments later I was aware of them removing my shirt. The sorcerer stopped his shuffling and approached me with a small pot of ointment. This smelled surprisingly sweet as he smeared some across my forehead and down my nose. He walked round me shaking a bunch of leaves, brushing them over my limbs and down my back.

My senses were spinning by this time but the hands holding my arms stopped me from falling. Strange visual effects appeared. In the darkness, the lanterns danced before my eyes, flaring and swinging, like bright sparklers being waved around by children. Bright colours joined the light display and sounds became muted, as though I was hearing them down a long tube.

Without warning, things began whirling around me. It was as if a flock of small birds was whizzing round my head, screaming, squawking and whistling. I wanted to put my arms up and bat them away but the strong hands held me. Moments later, I felt a great churning sensation in my guts and I thought I was going to be sick, but the vomit never came. My guts continued to churn and gurgle while my head spun and demons flew aerobatics around me. Some were brightly coloured, many were misty and ethereal, others dark and menacing. But for all their apparent menace, none did me any harm I was aware of.

Soon I was floating and vaguely realised I had been lifted to my feet. The sorcerer was no longer shuffling round me and his chanting had ceased. I tried to look round but couldn't see him or his table of fetish tools. Two shadowy figures supported me while more hands removed the rest of my clothing.

As I realised I was standing naked in front of all these people, my attention was distracted by two nubile and scantily clad young women putting a large bowl of water on the ground in front of me. They began washing me with wet cloths. One of them produced a bar of soap. Once again I smelt the strong orange scent. It was a scent that was to haunt and inspire me.

I didn't have time to think about the smell; the washers were becoming intimate, leaving no part of my anatomy unwashed, from my head to the soles of my feet. It was a muddling experience, with the whirling spirits – I now recognised them as that – still zooming around and appearing to pass straight through the two girls who were washing me. My guts were still doing tangos and my throat was too numb to utter a sound, leaving me at their mercy – and yet I didn't feel unsafe. Had I been less under the influence of Akgbegeyan's potions, I might have thoroughly enjoyed myself.

The girls withdrew and the sorcerer stood in front of me again. Holding a smoking pot, he blew across the top of it, directing a stream of smoke into my face. I wanted to flinch and turn away but something made me hold steady and keep my eyes open. They began to smart badly, but I chewed my tongue and stood still.

With a razor blade, he cut into my left breast and as the blood flowed he inserted five thorns to hold the sides of the cut together. I was only dimly aware of what he was doing and felt nothing. Not understanding the purpose of the cut, I stood and let it happen. Surprisingly, although the blood had flowed freely, it stopped the moment he inserted the thorns and wiped away what had run down my chest.

While Akgbegeyan was cutting a hole in my chest, two women had come up behind me and begun rubbing palm oil into my skin. They started at the top, massaging it into my scalp and combing it through my hair. While this was going on, the sorcerer gave me another potion to drink from an old smoked gourd. This one tasted both sweet and sharp at the same time but had no immediate effect, at least not on my consciousness. As one of the women prodded me to lift my foot, I looked down and realised I was very aroused. Nobody seemed to be taking any notice. Before I could give it further consideration, a burning sensation started where the cut had been made in my chest, followed by an unfamiliar flow of warmth which rushed out from there to every part of my body. It felt as if boiling water had been injected through the cut into my blood system and was circulating. My ears were hot and throbbing and there was a sharp tingling sensation all over my skin.

Hernan told me later it was the spirits having a look inside me. The cut was a doorway to let them in. Rubbing my body with oil helped them move freely inside me. It all sounded bizarre explained like this, yet it made sense in the context of their beliefs.

Before the oiling was finished, I felt very strange. My hearing was unaffected and I was aware of what was going on around me, but the rest of me belonged to someone else. The sorcerer approached again, waving a stick with a bright orange light on the end. It glowed brightly, describing bright arcs in the night air. It was only when it connected with my flesh that I realised it was an iron bar, and it was very hot.

He jabbed my left shoulder and there was a slight fizzing sound accompanied by the acrid smell of burning flesh. Several seconds later the drugged nerves in my system transmitted the pain to my brain and I felt the shock. My numbed throat stopped me crying out or I would have screamed. But, while the response was there, no sound came.

I heard humming in my ears and realised dimly that it was the people around me watching. They were murmuring comments about what had happened and how I had responded. This was an initiation and they were there to witness it. Had I known in advance what was going to happen, I wondered whether I would have allowed myself to be dragged into it. Then I remembered that Hernan had been telling me what to expect moments before it had begun.

Slowly things began to return to normal. The whirling shadows round me diminished and faded to nothing. Words and phrases spoken by watchers became more distinguishable and I turned to look at the two men holding me upright as sensation slowly returned to my feet and hands.

The sorcerer and his accoutrements had vanished. From somewhere behind me, Hernan's voice informed me that the ritual was ended. A woman's voice called out loudly from nearby. I turned to look at her and recognised Bejania, one of Djigénama's daughters, standing beside me.

"What are you going to do with that?" she demanded, pointing at my manhood. "Is it going to be wasted?" With returning sensation I could feel it throbbing and wondered the same thing myself.

"You are the only one who is free to use him," her mother replied.

I didn't understand what Djigénama meant, but got the gist when Bejania took hold of my arm and pulled me towards her hut. Even though normal sensation was beginning to resume in the rest of my body, my drug-befuddled brain was still not clear enough to resist as she pushed me inside, down onto the mat and swiftly shed her own clothing. A hurricane lamp gave just enough light for me to see as Bejania produced a packet of condoms. What followed was purely animal and, as my bodily functions returned to normal, great fun.

In the early hours I woke to find Bejania lying half across me, her head on my chest. Her two small children must have sneaked in during the night, for they lay close alongside. I disentangled myself, picked up my shorts that someone had placed just inside the door and headed towards the river for a wake-up wash. I had no idea what the implications of the previous night's events were and whether I now had commitments and obligations to fulfil. I needed urgently to find Hernan or Patrice.

Hernan was nowhere to be seen, but I did find Patrice who was happy to explain things to me. He told me I was now a member of Djigénama's family and therefore of the community. This meant that suggestions I might make for the project were likely to receive a better hearing than those of an outsider. It also meant that I always had a home and a family to support and help me whenever I was in the village. It was taken for granted that I was going to help with the laundry project and my assistance with that had already been accepted. Feeding Kebu the previous evening had been seen as behaving like a family member. The adoption was a way of recognising that.

"What about the initiation?"

"That was necessary for you to become part of the family. Our children are just children until they have been initiated. After that they are adults and become part of the family."

"And Bejania?"

"She is a widow. She has not had a man for two years since her husband was killed. Do not think badly of her for what she does."

"Do I now have obligations?"

"Not unless you want to. She is free to choose. Any other woman is restricted by taboos. She may not use another woman's man, but you are both free. Enjoy your fun."

Patrice and his grandson, Iube.

He made no mention of his fear the day before when I caught the pangolin, so I assumed he had decided I was nothing to do with his vile god, Simelenkele.

It was all highly surreal.

When I asked him about the condom, he laughed. "When the missionary was here, he taught us that we should use condoms to have sex for fun. They stop diseases. Only do it without if you are trying to make babies. All the woman have them."

It was an interesting perspective and very advanced thinking for the era.

The missionary had also been against female circumcision, the barbaric mutilation that was common in much of Africa. It had been obvious that Bejania had not been cut. Patrice told me the missionary had specifically taught them that cutting girls genitals was wrong. He told them the pleasure was God's gift and they should not destroy it. That was when the missionary told them to use condoms to avoid disease.

Since these things offered so much sexual freedom to both men and women, their community had evolved other customs to stop it getting out of hand. Generally everyone respected these rules and were faithful to their own wives or husband. That was why Bejania had needed release last night, but there was no ongoing obligation. If I wanted to take pleasure with her again and she agreed, that was our business.

Pondering this, I thought that missionary sounded very different from others I had met. But then the brand of Christianity these people practised was unlike any other I had seen. It made me wonder how Western Pentecostalists would view it. As deviant, I suspected, unable to imagine a Western pastor accepting the sorcerer and his propitiation of forest spirits alongside God. But for these people – the Lord be praised – it worked. Who was I to say they were wrong?

18 ~ Clean water

WHEN I WALKED UPRIVER to look at the pool where we intended to install the filter, I was surprised to find it a hive of activity. There must have been at least twenty people busy dragging out the accumulated debris and tipping it into the river to let the current carry it away. They had already cut back the overhanging vegetation around the edge of the pool, and work was in progress to clear the track so trucks would be able to get down to deliver the stone and sand.

Folomé was directing the activity and making a good job of it. The speed with which these villagers had got themselves organised was impressive. Elsewhere this would have taken weeks to organise, but this project had become a community affair and everyone stood to gain from it. Even the old hag was there, communing with the water spirits to ensure they would not object.

It surprised me that the pool had never become a swimming place for the village children. It was protected from the swift current of the river and had sloping banks so anyone could get in and out of the water with ease. A large tree overhung the pool and would have been an ideal place to hang a rope. Something like that always makes a great plaything for children. Not just children; I had seen adults getting as much pleasure from a swing – I might have tried it once or twice myself. At least its use for a water filter would be no disruption to other established uses.

Asiakunu told me the pool had been dug before living memory and nobody knew why it was not used. An old story told that children used to swim there, but one day a crocodile killed several of them. At least that's what the villagers assumed. When they had called their children in the evening, five were missing; they found only the head and arms of one and the legs and feet of another. The other three had vanished. Since that day, nobody dared go near the pool, believing it was cursed or haunted.

Looking at the river, I thought it unlikely that any crocodile had ever been near the place. The current was strong and crocodiles avoid fast flowing water like this. The story was rooted in the dim and distant past, long before the missionary had come here. It sounded far more likely that the children had been victims of a Voodoo sacrifice, with parts of each victim being consigned to the river and carried away by the current. This place was, after all, close to where Voodoo originated and a number of sacrificial cults remained active in the area, regardless of official prohibition.

When the pool was free of debris, we realised the middle of it was silted up and not deep enough for the filter, so we would have to excavate a six-foot-wide circle to an additional depth of two feet. This hole would then be partly filled with stones when the Highways Department truck delivered them, and the collecting box would be placed among those before being covered with more stone. After that a foot-thick layer of sand would be spread across the whole pool, leaving the water about three feet deep. Folomé and I had agreed to install a chain link barrier across the entrance from the river to stop further debris from being swept in. The villagers would need to clear this from time to time, but I felt confident that they would manage.

Digging out the extra clay became a chain operation. As one group dug it out, another group removed the clay in baskets, carried it ashore and piled it well back from the bank. It could be used later for building maintenance, repairs around the village or even making pots. There is always a good use for clay in Africa. The environment is humid and fairly wet, even in the dry season. Houses in Dogbo-Itémé needed continual maintenance and plastering their walls with clay was a continuous activity. With the volume of rainfall here, even the wide overhanging eaves didn't stop the walls suffering the effects of tropical rain. This clay would not go to waste.

It took us four days to prepare the pool and widen the track to allow two trucks to deliver the stones and sand. When the materials were delivered it took another gang effort to tip the stones into the bottom of the new hole and then it was my turn to wade in and install the filter collecting box. The take-off tube was already attached, and once I'd placed the adapted drum in position with a pile of stones over the top to hold it steady, we spread the next layer. It was a long job. Baskets of sand were passed from hand to hand and tipped into the pool, starting in the centre and spreading outwards. The water quickly turned muddy so we had to work by feel, raking it level below the surface. Some understood better than others what we were doing, but everyone was keen to join in.

With the sand laid, the filter was nearly ready to work. All we had to do was to connect the pipe to the pump and start pumping. Opinions varied about how the pump should be installed but in the end common sense prevailed and the villagers decided on a good concrete base with a roof over it. Building the base meant another couple of days' delay before we got the system working, but that was a small price to pay after all the effort that had already gone into the project.

We had some leftover sand and stone to make the concrete for the pump house. All we needed was a sack of cement, which we also got from the Highways Department. Two days later, it was done and the pump was installed. One of the village carpenters made a wooden framework over it and others brought palm leaves from the forest to thatch the roof.

We found a slight problem when it came to connecting the collecting box to the pump: the semi-rigid hose was too short. Someone had got their measurements wrong when they were positioning the pump base and we needed another fifteen feet of tubing. We were about to cut a bit off the output pipe that would deliver water to the laundry, but then realised that if we did this, that pipe would not reach. There was nothing for it but to go to town and buy more tubing.

DRIVING TO THE TOWN with Folomé gave us time to discuss how we could make water available down in the village as well as at the laundry site. There seemed to be no easy solution. The pump we had was powerful enough to lift water from the pool and push it as far as the laundry rocks, but it was the same distance again to the village. The ideal solution would be to get a large tank and install it half way, to use as a header tank. Whenever the laundry didn't need the flow, it would be diverted into the tank. Water could then be piped to the village by gravity through a pipe with a smaller bore.

Nearing the town, we came upon a road accident. A lorry had run off the road and overturned. A noisy crowd was milling about, holding up the traffic. Folomé leaned out of the window to ask what had happened and whether anyone had been hurt. He discovered the lorry was a 'honey wagon' – that's how the local night soil tankers were known – which had had a blowout and drifted off the road. It hit a culvert abutment and tipped over into the ditch. The cab was smashed and the tank had a huge dent in the side, but miraculously the driver had escaped unhurt and nobody else had been involved.

As we drove on, I wondered if anyone would bother recovering the vehicle and repairing it. A dent to the tank wouldn't matter, as long as it still held liquid without leaking. It might have been a sewage carrier, but there had to be a way to clean the thing out thoroughly and get rid of the smell. This could solve our most pressing problem and get water to the village. I would have to make enquiries.

The man at John Holt's sold us the last hundred feet of two-inch tubing in his stock and threw in a connector as a bonus because we had bought so much. We also bought a roll of one-inch plastic tubing. After stowing our purchases in the Land Rover, we drove to the Hygiene Department depot, where the honey wagons were based. The manager was scuttling about like a demented parrot, squawking instructions here, harrying fitters there, urgently needing to get wagons back on the road, and haranguing drivers who cheated on their fuel records. He barely had time to speak to us, but stopped and paid attention when I mentioned the wagon we had seen in the ditch.

"That's all I need," he complained. "We have vehicles breaking down all the time because the government is too mean to spend any money on spare parts. We never get new tyres and the roads are so bad the tyres we have get shredded in no time. I have six wagons waiting for repair and now this one is smashed. It can stay in the ditch and rot, for all I care."

Oh what music this outburst was to my ears! It was nearly the end of the working day, so I invited the manager to come and eat with us, offering beer with the meal as an enticement. He agreed and waddled away to issue a last string of orders to his drivers and mechanics. Ten minutes later, as we were sitting in a local eatery with frosted bottles of beer in front of us, I floated an idea. If he could write off the crashed vehicle and remove it from his inventory, I was willing to buy the wreck from him and pay cash for it. He could use the money to buy spare parts for his other wagons. I was sure his paperwork was complicated enough to lose the wreck.

"You'd have to remove it yourself," he said.

"That's understood."

"And it's full of shit."

"Perhaps we could hire one of your wagons for an hour and pump it out," I suggested. "Paying cash for the hire, of course."

I saw him warm to the idea as he sucked cool beer from his bottle. Our food arrived and we ate together, talking about the iniquities of officialdom, drinking more beer and avoiding the subject of the crashed honey wagon. With the third round of beer, he returned to the topic.

"That's an old truck, but it's still worth good money. You can have it for 250,000 CFA," he announced. "And 5,000 to hire a wagon to pump it out."

I did a quick mental calculation. At 630 CFA to the pound, that was about four hundred pounds sterling. To buy a tank that would supply a whole village, it was a snip. "Agreed," I said without consulting Folomé, and held out my hand to shake on the deal. He shook it without hesitation. If necessary I would pay for it from my discretionary fund. At least this way the rest of the project could go ahead and the whole community stood to gain from it.

We agreed to meet at the crash site early the next morning. He would bring another wagon to pump out the tank, I would bring the cash and, as a bonus, he could send someone to take spares off the truck once I had got it back to Dogbo-Itémé as it would not need to be drivable once it was there. It was the tank that was important to us.

We dropped him off outside the gate of his depot and headed back to the village in a buoyant mood.

THREE DAYS LATER, Folomé started the pump. We used the first flow it delivered to wash down and thoroughly scour the old honey wagon. Apart from the huge dent in the side, the tank was in remarkably good condition. After four rinses and a scrub with bleach, it hardly smelled at all. We filled it with fresh water, dosed it heavily with chlorine salts and left it to stand overnight. I was confident that after this it would be hygienic enough for the village to use as a water tank and any residual aroma would gradually dissipate.

Before refilling it and adding the chlorine salts, we replaced the gate valve on the back with a conventional tap. This would let the village women fill their domestic water cans easily. To begin with, the water was cloudy with river silt, but after a final flush and once the filter was working properly, the water would be sparkling clean. Meanwhile, it could be used by the laundry. Just from being drawn through the sand, it was already cleaner than the river water they had been using before, and the ladies remarked on how much cleaner it got their washing.

The river water still had a distinctly rusty colour, but gradually, as the pump continued to operate, the biological mat formed on the surface of the sand. After sixteen hours, the water arriving at the laundry was sparkling bright and held only the faintest tinge of colour. The villagers gave praise to the Lord every time they filled a bowl with this miraculous fluid. Even the old hag by the river looked pleased, muttering that the water spirits had been kind to give up their water so freely.

Asiakunu and Djigénama, the instigators of the scheme, where ecstatic. The freely available supply for the village was very popular. The women could now draw their domestic supplies from the old honey wagon tank instead of having to carry it half a mile from the river. And when we had another tube connected with a standpipe, they would have a supply on the edge of the village. The village artisans had shown themselves competent to look after the equipment involved.

MY VISIT WAS COMING TO an end and I felt sad to be leaving. These villagers had a strange but interesting mixture of cultures. They were enthusiastic, forward-looking and free-thinking, willing to invest heavily in their own future and remarkably united as a community. Dogbo-Itémé was an enclave of happy success in an area rife with demonic beliefs and practices, where life was still marginal and tribal rivalries were common.

Apart from all the cultural things I had learned at Dogbo-Itémé, I had discovered some practical skills for life in the forest and acquired a new perspective on the way people related to modern technology. I had gained inspiration from their use of locally available ingredients and materials and now had knowledge I could take on to use in other places.

The inclusion of orange essence in the soap had been the most significant of these as it gave me an idea for what might be possible with the wild oranges far away in the south-west corner of Mali.

THE NIGHT BEFORE MY departure was noisy, musical and boozy. The villagers needed little excuse to start singing hymns and songs. The Lord received a lot of thanks and praise for my visit, and for my adoption into Djigénama's family. I got little sleep that night.

Having packed my Land Rover the previous afternoon, I slipped out of the village as dawn was lightening the sky, waved off by only Asiakunu, Djigénama and Bejania, while everyone else still slept. Hernan had managed to drag himself from his bed, but not from sleep. Later that day, when I dropped him off at his father's house, he couldn't remember leaving the village. He had been slumped in the passenger seat all the way back to Lokossa.

PART 3

DEAL WITH
A DEVIL

A strange figure, swathed in heavy raffia skirts and an all-enveloping dark green top... (Photo courtesy of Tim Butcher)

19 ~ Improvisation

IT TOOK ME A WEEK TO get home to Anéhigouya, the village where I lived in northern Upper Volta. There were several other development projects to visit along the way. It was important to check their progress regularly and I arrived home brimming with ideas. My aeroplane was now ready to fly again. I made a two-day trip by Mobylette to Bobo-Dioulasso to pick it up. Leaving the Land Rover in the village meant it would still be available as ground transport when I returned to base.

Back in the air, with my Mobylette safely stowed behind the co-pilot's seat, I decided to make a small diversion into Mali to Kofoli and visit the well school. I tried to visit regularly and, with a course nearing completion, I wanted to see the graduating students before they went home to their own countries. We had people from five different West African countries on this course and it was important to keep in touch. Apart from anything, they needed to be told about the equipment that had been provided in their absence, ready for their use when they got home.

Being this close, I took the opportunity to drop in on Father Bernhardt at the Bula Farm School as well. He had planted several

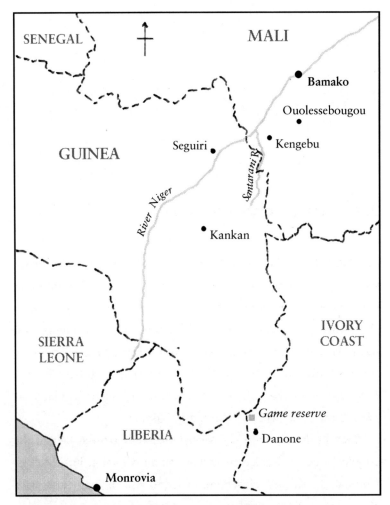

South-west Mali, Ivory Coast, Guinea and Liberia

hundred citrus trees on the farm and I wanted to pick his brains about the wild groves I had found in the southwest. Endlessly inventive and practical, he was a man I was sure would have useful ideas to share.

Over lunch, we discussed the trees I had found and potential uses of the wild fruit. We concluded that the only part which might have any use worth pursuing was the zest or, more particularly, the oil in the zest. Its intense aroma might be of interest as a scent additive. Our discussion faltered over how to collect the oil.

Father Bernhardt had Beethoven's 'Eroica' Symphony playing on his old windup gramophone. We sat and absorbed the music, hoping it would inspire us. Listening to the glorious chords pouring from the big brass horn on the phonograph, an idea struck me. Father Bernhardt must have had the same idea at the same moment as we looked at one another, then at the phonograph, and grinned. A needle could pierce the oil sacs on the fruit skin. If the fruit was spun like an old cylinder phonograph, the needle could be moved across and cover the whole surface. It was simple! Centrifugal force should do the rest.

Making it work would be a little more difficult, but with the help of a skilled engineer, we were confident it could be done. After scribbling a few essential points on paper and drawing rough diagrams of how it might work, we went for a walk around the farm. Father Bernhardt gave me a basket of fresh oranges and paw-paws to take home. This had been a most fruitful visit in more ways than one.

In the end, I didn't fly straight back to Anéhigouya, but made a small diversion to the airport at Bobo-Dioulasso to talk to the engineer who had done the overhaul on my plane. Albert Daggia was a Hungarian who had somehow ended up in this African backwater. If he didn't know where I could get a mechanism made that would do what I needed, he would certainly have the means in his workshop to construct something. It needed to be simple and robust as it would be operated by people with no mechanical knowledge or training, and it would need to be able to process many thousands of oranges, as the volume of oil in each skin was very small.

Albert was intrigued with the idea, but curious to know why I wanted to extract the oil from orange skins.

"For its scent," I explained, and told him how I had seen the soap-makers in Dogbo-Itémé using the zest to perfume their soap, and was planning to investigate whether any perfume manufacturers in France would be interested in a supply of wild orange oil. In anticipation of demand wherever it might come from, I needed a means of providing a supply. What I wanted Albert to invent was a mechanism to extract the stuff, ideally in commercial quantities.

"So is there money in this?" his interest quickened.

"Only if it can be made viable. Can you help me?"

"Come back in a week." He turned away, his mechanical mind already focussed on the problem.

I RETURNED TO ANÉHIGOUYA where the team sinking a new borehole had just finished and was preparing to move to another village fifteen miles away. This meant our village now had two good wells and a water supply for the future. The drilling team had come from the well school and would be training a new team of drillers on the next borehole.

The Anéhigouya borehole used a percussion drill as it only needed to go down a hundred feet to reach the aquifer. The one in the next village needed to go much deeper and there was a layer of hard rock to go through. For this, the team would be using the more powerful rotary drilling rig. I wanted to be around when they started, to check on the instructors as much as on the students' progress.

It was ten days before I got back to see Albert Daggia. He had used the time well and had made a smart looking piece of clockwork. It worked like a rotisserie with a tracking arm. A gramophone needle donated by Father Bernhardt was fitted into the end of the tracking arm. Mounted on a threaded bar, geared to the spindle by cog wheels, the arm carried the needle across as the fruit spun. The weight of the head holding the needle against the fruit's surface would be enough to puncture all the little oil sacks in the skin without ripping the skin to shreds. Centrifugal force would flick the oil outwards to be collected in a container. He demonstrated it with a rubber ball the size of a small orange. The needle scratched a fine line across most of the surface.

It was an ingenious device. The only problem was that it had no container. Any oil released would be flicked outwards and blown away on the breeze. Albert had thought of this. He had constructed a light alloy frame to carry sheets of glass. This would collect the oil and allow it to dribble down to a funnel with a bottle underneath. All I had to do was find someone to cut the glass and stick it into the frame.

I asked him why he had hadn't used sheet metal and he explained that the oil was likely to be slightly acidic and might react with the metal. As it was, he had anodised all the parts of the mechanism to reduce corrosion. He had also considered the possibility that contact with metal might taint the oil and affect its smell.

He seemed to have thought of everything and then refused payment. All he would let me pay for was the new material he had used, which amounted to very little as most of it had been scrap. He suggested that if I could make this crazy idea work I should buy his wife a bottle of expensive perfume and we'd be quits.

I took the contraption into town to find a glazier.

With the glass panels fitted, and a set of spare pieces in case of breakage carefully packaged, I headed home with the machine. In the market in Ouahigouya, I bought a box of oranges to play with, thinking our village children could eat the fruit after it had been through the machine. The needle was only supposed to scratch the surface enough to release oil from the pores; the flesh would still be perfectly edible. Oranges were certain to be popular with the children, an exciting addition to a plain and stodgy diet.

Although I began conducting my trials in the privacy of my own courtyard, nothing remains secret in an African village for long. People always know what others in the community are doing. It was my next door neighbour's youngest son, Akubu, who let the secret out. He often climbed onto the flat roof of his father's house so he could observe what was going on in my compound.

Before I had managed to scrape more than half a dozen oranges, a visitor scratched at my gate and clapped his hands seeking entry. Not surprisingly, it was Braheem Ouaganyandi, the village blacksmith. He was fascinated by anything mechanical or made of metal. The idea that I might have a new machine in my compound drew him there with the strength of a powerful electromagnet. He watched it working, marvelling at how smoothly the arm travelled across the fruit and how close together the scratched lines made by the passage of the needle were, ensuring that every cell was pierced. He also loved the sound of the gently whirring clockwork motor. I'm sure that he would have taken the whole thing to pieces to understand how it worked if I had let him.

When I had tried it out on twenty oranges, I gave a basket of scratched fruit to Akubu and asked him share them with the other children. I promised him more the next day. With the sun going down, he wouldn't be able to see much more tonight anyway, so he went off happily and I turned my attention to making food.

Soon after that, another hand scratched at my gate. The scratch was familiar and moments later the Wa-Wa man pushed open the gate and insinuated himself into my courtyard. I shouldn't have been surprised; he had a nose for anything new and invariably knew when there was an opportunity to share my food. But I couldn't understand why he never opened the gate properly and always sneaked in sideways as if by so doing he might not be noticed by some guardian spirit. I never had the nerve to ask him in case I learned something I would rather not have known.

He had shared my evening meal on many occasions and was always curious about what I was doing. He might have been the village witch-doctor, but he had also become a good friend, one whom I trusted completely.

There had not been time during my last sojourn in the village to discuss my visit to south-west Mali and the discovery of the orange trees. His presence this evening gave me the chance to ask if he could think of any spiritual reason why the fruit was so bitter and why the trees had been abandoned.

The people in the region must have had a very strong reason to abandon an important food source. It couldn't have been as simple as the fruit's bitterness. Things like that can be overcome. In regions where cassava was the staple, the majority of the crop tasted bitter, laden with prussic acid. It required extensive washing to remove this before it could be eaten. There was a sweet variety, but it was far less commonly grown, and where it was, it was often pillaged by wild animals and other humans alike. It was also more prone to diseases. Farmers grew the toxic variety, even though it gave their women far more work and required patience to prepare. The bitter variety also gave bigger tubers and better yields, which might have had something to do with their choice.

So why hadn't people found a use for these bitter citrus fruits? Was there a spiritual taboo? If so, how did it stop the wild beasts from eating the fruit, leaving it solely to the wasps and hornets?

We talked about this for a long while, and the Wa-Wa man had fun trying out the machine. He dipped his finger in the oil that came off, sniffing at it with interest.

"People buy that?" he asked. I had already told him what I proposed to try and do with it.

"Yes. On its own it's not much use, but combined with other essences, it's used to make sweet smelling perfumes that Western women crave."

He looked doubtful.

"You use different ingredients in your potions and medicines," I reminded him. "Each has its own properties. When they're mixed, they unite to make the medicine. It's the same principle."

A smile crept across his craggy face. "Perhaps I should have a new job making perfumes for European ladies," he grinned.

"I don't think they would appreciate the smell of some of your potions," I said and we both laughed.

The Wa-wa man could think of no spiritual taboo to prevent the people from exploiting the fruit, but suggested a number of things I should ask the local sorcerers about before plunging into the project too deeply. Meanwhile, I had a machine that would extract the oil at least in quantities sufficient to send out as samples, should anyone want them.

20 ~ Searching for spirits

OTHER LARGE PROJECTS HAD priority and it was another month before I was able to go back to south-west Mali. Summer was at its height and the sun was blazing down as I left Anéhigouya for the long bumpy drive. I had decided to go in the Land Rover since there was not yet a cleared area of bush to let me land the plane, plus I had the machine to take.

That year the rains had been generous and turned the countryside lush and green, completely transforming it from the dusty landscape I had travelled across during my last visit. It took four days to get to the region as some of the streams of the Niger headwaters were in spate and now ran as raging torrents. They might only be a few yards wide, but still needed to be treated with respect, for the force of the water was rolling huge stones down the narrow gullies. A light Land Rover would have stood no chance.

The land in Mali was clothed in generous new growth. Again I wondered why it wasn't more densely populated. Patches of elephant grass were already ten feet high and the ground vegetation was burgeoning. The soil was obviously fertile; logic said crops should have done well here. Yet I saw few proper farms, only occasional patches of millet and sorghum. This time however there were even more birds flitting between the bushes. The transformation was so complete it was tempting to wonder if I had come to the right place, but a few prominent rock outcrops confirmed my navigation and I headed onwards.

It was late when I reached Ouelessebougou. The dirty, ramshackle town looked unchanged, except for new crowns of greenery around some of the compounds where fresh poles stuck into the ground to make fences had taken root and sprouted leaves. The little shade they cast was always welcome in summer, and when the new branches were woven together, they strengthened the palisade.

My return attracted a little attention, first from a crowd of children who gathered to stare, then from people I had met last time I was here. They made me welcome, offered food, and I had no trouble finding somewhere to spend the night. It was when they asked me where I was going that I realised I had never asked the name of the village where Nasia and Ayenu lived. I had taken them back there, spent a day with them and their families, and didn't even know the name of the place.

This didn't seem to matter as the bush telegraph had been active. News of their return from the dead had spread throughout the countryside, even as far as this outlandish place. The moment Nasia's name was mentioned they knew where I was going and I received helpful directions from several individuals. Inevitably they conflicted. If I had tried to follow any of them, goodness knows where I would have ended up. There was nothing for it but to trust my memory and the few scrappy marks I had made on my map. I felt sure that if I could find the Sankarani River, it would be easy enough to get back to the right place.

It didn't occur to me that when the rains came, the Sankarani completely changed its character and was unrecognisable compared to the lazy canal I had visited before. I drove around in circles for two days before chance brought an encounter with a man from the village. He recognised me and offered to show me the way. With his guidance it took less than an hour to find the village.

We received a warm welcome from Nasia and Ayenu. Both were in good health, a far cry from the state I had originally found them in. Now, despite their advanced age, they were full of life and vigour. Nasia looked even more wrinkled than before, but still had a bright twinkle in her eyes. There was life aplenty within. Although I suspected she already knew the answers, she quizzed me in detail about why I had come back, and was very interested in what I told her about the orange oil. I gave her a bar of soap from Dahomey, which she lifted often to her nose and sniffed while we talked.

I noticed that Ayenu sat quietly listening but offered no comment. From our previous encounter, I knew that whenever he did this there was something important going on in his mind. After a few minutes, I asked him directly if he could tell me anything about the orange groves and why the fruit was so bitter. He smiled slightly and took his time to answer.

Eventually he told me the trees were inhabited by bad spirits which had migrated there from the south. It happened many years ago, before white men came to the area. A long way from here, there had been a terrible disease which carried off many people. The medicine men were unable to treat it. Devils in that country drove the medicine men out, saying they were no use, and not fit to live among their own people. These devils were men of the Poro cult, and they had taken over. Poro, I knew, is a secret society whose members use very strong magic. Those devils are best avoided, Ayenu told me. The medicine men who were driven out came north, but they were cursed. They brought with them just enough to survive. They settled and formed a small community where the orange trees now grow. They planted crops and fruit trees, but within a few years the crops had turned against them. The trees grew but gave fruit so bitter that not even the wild animals could eat it. These were the trees I had found.

In time, the people who had planted them died out. The crops all went wild and the stalks of their millet grew monstrously tall and deformed. They still grow as great clumps of elephant grass, with knife-edged leaves and stems as thick as Ayenu's wrist and twice as tall as me.

All these things happened because of the curses the Poro men had put on their medicine men before they chased them away. There are many bad stories about the Poro, he told me. In their own country, after the great sickness had passed, those who remained turned to evil practices and human sacrifice had become common. Since those days, the sorcerers of his people wanted nothing to do with the devils from the south. The medicine men who came died of hunger, but their spirits still linger among the trees.

If I wanted to use that fruit, Ayenu told me, the curse must first be removed. "Etu cannot do this," he said.

If I wanted this project to proceed, it meant I would have to venture into the land of the devils, across the border in Guinea or beyond. None of his people would dare go there.

Beyond meant Liberia, where I had already made one brief visit. Poro was indeed a strong cult in that region and horror stories abounded, although most people were too terrified ever to speak about the secret society or what it did. In the early years of the twentieth century, several American missionaries had tried to investigate Poro. All had failed to achieve more than a superficial encounter, and none was able to provide substantiated facts.

This was going to be a difficult hurdle to surmount. I wished Ayenu had told me all this before things had got this far. It was a bit late now. I had made a machine and, in my mind at least, had committed myself to harvesting orange oil and making something of my crazy idea.

Maybe I would have to go and ask a devil to release the curse.

FROM THE VILLAGE, IT WAS easy enough to find my way back to the stick hut. It looked as derelict as it had four months earlier. The acacia stump I had used as an anvil had been attacked by white ants. Half of it was eaten away; but otherwise everything looked the same. I was surprised that termites hadn't invaded the stick hut, but then realised it was probably protected by a charm.

It is easy for people who don't live with African magic to pooh-pooh such ideas, but I had seen them work too many times before to discount this. The hut was, after all, a sacred place; one of transition between two synchronous worlds, where men die and ancestors are born. It is right that it should be protected until it had served its purpose, and that might span many years and multiple transitions. I still wasn't sure if it was only special people who were brought here, or whether anyone who was dying would do so here. One day Nasia and Ayenu might be brought here again.

The stick hut was only a short distance to the orange grove but the land was broken by numerous gullies and streams, so it wasn't a five-minute drive. I parked fifty yards from the trees and approached on foot, looking carefully for fetish signs that might indicate the place was protected.

I found none. The grass and small bushes all around it were normal. Sunbirds flitted between blossoms, harvesting nectar and emitting shrill cheeps and twiddles. A buzz of apian activity somewhere in the canopy told me there were bees there too. In the grass, crickets scraped their incessant rasping song, and I noticed the tracks and droppings of at least two bush rodents before I reached the first trees.

Not all the trees had fruit on them, but most did. Many also carried blossom and the scent of it was heavy on the air. I saw a few parasitic orchids and wondered how many more there might be. These were not the big flashy blooms of cultivated orchids but small stems with many little, rather plain flowers on them. They had no strong scent I could detect, but were popular with at least one species of little black beetle. Lots of these were flitting from flower to flower. Pollination was well assured here.

I rambled through the grove for three-quarters of an hour, looking at the trees and other plants, trying to find signs of human activity, all the time keeping a weather eye open for a charm or fetish. There was nothing out of the ordinary, so I started a grid count of the trees. They grew somewhat randomly so this was not easy, but I came up with an estimate of 490 trees. Most of them carried at least four hundred two-inch fruits. Some weeks later when we counted them properly and numbered the trees, there turned out to be 506.

Leaving these trees, I drove round to scout for a route southwards and saw several other stands. It seemed that orange trees were quite common here. This was good news because from my first calculations it looked as if it would be necessary to process over seven hundred oranges to get a measurable quantity of oil from the skins. For the project to be viable and interest a Parisian perfume house, it would have to be able to produce the oil in commercial quantities. That meant a lot of oranges.

I scouted six more groves that day, finding good fruit in all of them and no visible signs of magical protection. With this clear in my mind, I went in search of the sorcerer from Nasia's village, to ask his advice.

Etu Ikemongoutlu was a slender man who stooped as if carrying the weight of the world on his shoulders. It was probably scoliosis that was bending him, but even bent he was taller than most men in the village. Nasia had already warned him that I would come to seek his advice, and he therefore showed no surprise when I made my request. I had forgotten that the old woman was a seer.

He knew all about my visit to the orange groves even though I had told no one what I had seen or what I had thought. He also knew what Ayenu had told me and agreed that the curses must be removed before trying to do anything with the fruit. He couldn't do it; he didn't know what curses had been used or what protection the groves had on them and was unwilling to meddle in someone else's magic.

I remarked that I had not seen a single tree with the mark of an axe on it and he laughed, saying it would be a foolhardy man who tried to collect firewood from sacred or protected trees.

"But how do people know they are protected?" I asked.

"They have always been so. We all know this," he replied, as though the matter needed no explanation. Anything everybody knew is fact, even though nobody could say where that knowledge came from.

I asked in there could be something in the soil that made the fruit so bitter no man could eat it. He thought this unlikely but suggested a family of spirits might live in the trees. They didn't want anyone to use the fruit so they made it bitter to warn men off. Among people so open to superstitious suggestion, this could easily be the case.

After a long discussion, Etu agreed to go with me to see if he could detect any charms protecting the trees. He said he had never been there before, even though they were well within the range of his meanderings, but since Nasia had reassured him that a visit would have no unexpected or undesirable outcome for him, he let himself be persuaded.

As it turned out, the following morning Nasia decided she would come too. The three of us climbed into the Land Rover and set off early, before it got too hot.

Etu's flapping hand brought me to a stop two hundred yards from the first orange trees. He wanted to walk in so that he might see and feel any charms that had been laid around the area. Within a few yards he stopped and examined a small bush I had driven past the day before. I could see nothing unusual about the bush until he pointed out that it was not typical of the surrounding flora. The very fact of it's being out of place meant something to him, but then he was not only an initiate, but an adept in his craft. Such subtle signs were his speciality. Realisation of this fact gave me another fleeting glimpse into the esoteric world he took for granted and the rest of us ignored in our sublime ignorance. I resolved to pay more attention and learn from this man.

Etu walked on slowly, casting around for signs and soon stopped at a small patch of clear ground. To anyone else, this was just a patch of empty ground covering about a yard in diameter. To him it was significant. All around was rough grass and small bushes, but this patch stood out by being precisely circular and completely devoid of any growth.

I asked what caused this and Etu told me it was a spirit mark. Nothing could grow here. Was the spirit friendly? He didn't know. To find out, a divination would be needed, to invite the spirit to identify itself. He would explore more first before doing this. There might be other signs.

We walked on.

The Land Rover horn sounded behind us. I had forgotten Nasia was still sitting in the cab and now she wanted our attention so I walked back to her.

"There are spirits here," she told me as I opened the driver's door. "They are trapped by something and searching for a way out. I can feel them."

I looked back at Etu who had almost reached the trees. He was standing with his arms outstretched and I could hear him talking, but couldn't make out his words. It wouldn't have made any difference; he was speaking to the spirits and the words were a toneless jumble to human ears. But as I knew from other sorcerers I had met, it had great power in the right circles.

For almost fifteen minutes, Nasia and I waited, listening and looking. In the ways I had learned, I tried to open my own senses to any spiritual presence that might reveal itself. Suddenly the air felt chill and I had a sense of something rushing by me, but I saw nothing. Remembering the whirling forms I had encountered during my initiation in Dahomey, I wondered if any of the same spirits that inhabited that forest might also live in these trees. Were they tree spirits or forest dwellers? Did spirits travel far? Would they be benign or hostile? Many of those I had encountered before had a distinctly hostile, almost threatening quality about them. Others had touched me with fingers of silk, like comforting and reassuring friends. All had made distinct impressions which I could recall easily enough, and yet I had no words to describe them. They were simply identities I recognised. Such is the way of spirits.

As we waited, it seemed as if more and more forms began to congregate, whirling in the air with subliminal presence, some drifting, some zooming, creating an aerobatic chaos that disturbed the clear sunlit air. I was aware of them yet nothing was visible. It was only now that I began to understand the significance of the ritual I had endured in Dogbo-Itémé. Initiation, with the opening of the senses, gives the facility to participate in a little more of life than the mundane physical here and now. It takes a mind that has grown up with Africa fully to understand this.

I felt my left shoulder itching where the burn Akgbegeyan made with his hot iron rod had marked me. The burn had healed long ago, leaving only a round white mark the size of my thumbnail on my otherwise suntanned skin.

As I was to understand later, there are degrees of initiation and I was still a novice. Those who went to further levels faced stern and dramatic trials, tests that could kill, and levels of secrecy that make western spies look like amateurs.

Etu turned and motioned for me to accompany him as he walked among the trees. He reached out, stroking the branches and trunks of trees as we passed them. The tone of his mutterings sounded like enquiries; was he asking the names of spirits residing there? Or enquiring after the health of the trees themselves?

I looked more closely at the trees, realising that most of them were very old. They must have been here for many years, their fruit falling to the ground and rotting, consumed only by insects and microbes. Perhaps that, and the shadow cast by their canopies, was why little else grew on the ground. Maybe after all the rotten fruit had been absorbed by the ground the soil had become too acid.

I put a hand on Etu's arm to get his attention and asked if it would be all right to take a sample of the soil for testing. He shrugged and then nodded, seeing no reason why we shouldn't try every means of understanding this place. Using the knife from my belt I scraped a small sample into a plastic bag – I always had one in my pocket in those days – and folded it away to test when we got back to the Land Rover.

After a while, we returned to where Nasia was waiting. She was sitting on the front bumper, with her eyes closed but clearly not asleep. I took my testing kit from its storage locker in the back and tested my soil sample for ph. It came out at 5.3 which made it strongly acidic. I walked three hundred yards along the tracks our wheels had made as we approached and took another sample. This showed a value of 6.8, which was broadly neutral. It was an interesting contrast but far from conclusive, so I labelled the two bags, intending to do a more detailed analysis later, and stowed them with the test kit.

Etu wanted to visit some of the other groves, so we drove on, stopping to look at five different patches of trees before the heat became too oppressive. I took soil samples from each and from the open land between them. The result was the same: the soil in all the groves was markedly acid while that in the open bush it was neutral.

After six groves, Etu had seen enough. He wanted to return to the village and conduct a divination. He told me it was a good thing I had brought soil from the groves as these and the fruit we'd harvested from each one as we walked around would help him locate the spirits he called to speak. I had collected the soil with far more prosaic purposes in mind and had visions of them being frittered away by his divinations. He assured me the soil only needed to be present; his divination would not consume any part of it and I would still be able to carry out my tests.

There were nearly a hundred oranges in the back of the Land Rover by the time we got back to the village. I wanted to use them to try out the machine and see how much oil this number would produce. It would be the first live trial and could determine if the idea had any future or whether I had been chasing a fanciful dream. I told Etu how I was going to use them and he said I should wait and let him do the divination first. After that I could take the oranges outside the village to conduct my trial. He didn't want possessive spirits getting angry with his village.

I agreed to take them beyond the stick hut, to the spot where I had crashed on the anthill, and he seemed satisfied with this.

21 ~ Divination and trial

ON MY MAP, I SHOWED Etu the locations and relative positions of the different groves. He had never seen a map before and had difficulty making sense of the image on paper. He asked me to scratch an outline in the dirt outside his house and place three fruits from each group of trees on this in the positions they came from. Beside each pile of fruit I placed the soil from that grove and had started putting the open bush samples in the gaps between when he waved these away. He only wanted to call spirits from where the orange trees were, not from the surrounding countryside. My presence was not needed either; this was sorcerer's business.

I was hot and sticky after drawing his map in the dirt and populating it with the fruit and soil samples, so I pulled off my shirt to let the breeze cool me. The moment I did this, Etu grabbed my arm. Pointing at the white brand mark on my left shoulder, he asked how I had come by it. When I explained how the fetish priest had marked me in Dahomey, his eyes lit up and he said I should stay and help him with the divination after all.

He said he was confused among the orange trees as there had

been another presence beside him. It had never occurred to him that it might be me. White men don't normally understand spirits.

Nasia, who was sitting on an upturned pot nearby watching the preparations, smiled when he said this. "I told you he was open," she cackled. "Next time perhaps you'll listen to one who knows."

Etu looked uncomfortable and tried to ignore the jibe, but he kept glancing in her direction. There was a frisson of tension in the air as the two adepts manoeuvred for position and status. I hadn't realised this could matter but clearly it did. Etu was the sorcerer and diviner. Nasia was only a seer. The fact that she was probably twice as old as Etu didn't come into it; this was about roles and a very clear demarcation lay between the two.

While Etu was making his preparations I went and squatted down next to Nasia.

"Will he find the spirits that control the trees?" I asked.

"He has already found them. Now he must ask if the trees are tabu and seek permission to use them."

"Will he get this?"

"He will only learn how to ask for it. You will have to find the devil who holds the spirits in bondage."

"So why doesn't he just say so if you already know this?"

"I only see what will happen. He is the one who can tell you where to ask and how to do it. The sorcerer talks to the spirits. He must divine to understand the bondage."

It was hardly surprising that there was a lot of wisdom in this old bird's head. Much of her life may have been spent in a bush village, but there was no doubting that she had seen many things.

Etu was ready and stood in front of the scratched map with the piles of fruit and little bags of soil laid out. There was a different aura about him now; his arms were festooned with amulets he had not worn earlier. An animal skin was draped over his shoulders with the legs tied through the loop of a wooden ring with a small iron bell hanging in front of his chest. He had smeared his face and chest with ochre. Usually an undistinguished figure, he looked most impressive. Surely the spirits would see and take notice of him.

He motioned for me to stand beside him and smeared stripes of yellow paste down my chest with his fingers. I felt it scorch as he applied it and wondered if it was caustic. It was too late to worry as Etu began his call to the spirits, his arms held out towards the display of fruit on the ground in front of us.

I listened carefully and I couldn't understand a word, but his tone sounded like an invitation. Like music with a theme and variations, I began to recognise repetitions and guessed that each appealed to a different spirit. For some minutes nothing happened. All of a sudden there was motion above us. I looked up, seeing nothing, yet felt sure there was something there.

Etu continued his chant, slightly louder and more insistent. The feeling that we were not alone became stronger. Suddenly he flinched. Moments later something stabbed me in the side. Lifting my hand to the spot I found neither wound nor mark, just the pain as if a sharp stick had been thrust into me. Etu took an orange from the first pile, scraped it with his thumbnail and then wiped it over the point where I had felt the pain. The pain vanished as the scent of orange oil filled the sweaty afternoon air.

Soon after this I began to feel slightly dizzy. My vision became indistinct and Etu's figure seemed to waver as if distorted by heat haze. I shook my head to dispel the dizziness, but the fluttering shadows persisted. Some felt familiar yet I could see none of them nor identify their characteristics. My rational mind intruded and told me it was the product of heatstroke and dehydration, but I did nothing to alleviate this and continued standing there while Etu went on with his ritual.

He pointed to each pile of fruit in turn, dipping his finger tip in the bag of soil next to it and chanting in a different tone. His change of tone had slipped my notice and it occurred to me I wasn't paying proper attention. I was still new at this business and, without knowing what was happening or what was supposed to be happening, it was difficult to keep focussed.

Before I could get my mind back on track, it was all over. Etu wiped my face with a cloth and offered me a pot of water to drink, saying I could remove the bags of soil now and do what I wanted with them. He gathered up all the oranges, most of which were still green skinned, although they were ripe, and put them in my basket. Placing the basket in my hands, he told me to come back at sunset and he would explain what the spirits had told him.

He turned and disappeared inside his hut.

I was left bemused and slightly confused, unsure what to make of the whole business and wondering what sort of pronouncement he would make later. I suspected it would be vague and obscure; men like him are never very precise.

There were still two hours to sunset, so I took the soil samples back to the Land Rover and tested them. The ph values for soil from beneath the trees all came out at the same level, 5.3. I knew citrus trees like slightly acid soil, but this seemed a little extreme. Nevertheless, the trees were all healthy and laden with fruit and flowers, so it obviously wasn't a problem. The ph in the open bush varied between 6.6 and 7.1, so the surrounding countryside was unambiguously neutral. The only remaining question was whether the fruit trees had flourished in pockets of pre-existing acidity or whether it was produced by years of rotting windfalls. It seemed to be a mystery on a par with the one the sorcerer was trying to unravel, but I doubted he would be able to answer this one.

Citrus trees tend not to like high salinity, so that was my next test. Unfortunately the equipment I had with me gave only approximate results; a conclusive test would have to wait until I could get the samples to a properly equipped laboratory, but I could get some idea.

I ran the tests twice and by the time dusk was encroaching, I was sure the soil in the groves was more saline than in the open bush, but neither would be classed as highly saline. Among the trees, however, the salinity was a little above the level at which citrus trees grow best, yet they were healthy. Anomalies are going to be the norm here, I thought.

Frustrated by not getting a definite result, I made my way to the sorcerer's hut to hear what the spirits had told him. In the end it didn't really matter what the soil composition was; the trees were growing well and carried abundant fruit. It was the fruit I wanted, or rather the oil in the skin of that fruit. Tomorrow I would wind up the machine and try extracting some oil, to see if this project might theoretically work.

ETU WAS SITTING OUTSIDE his hut waiting for me. He accepted the packet of cigarettes I offered as I sat down, and lit one. Blowing out a long cloud of smoke, he looked at me with a doubtful expression on his face.

"There are many spirits in those trees," he began. "They are crying. They have been trapped for many years. Nobody has come to release them. Unless they are released, they will not allow anyone to use the fruit."

"Will they let me take enough oil from the fruit we have gathered to show that they could have a use?"

"You can take a little oil. The spirits have seen your soul. They know your intentions. But you cannot use the fruit. You must get the curse that binds them lifted."

"How do I do that?"

"You must find a devil who knows that magic. Ask him to break the curse."

"And where will I find this devil?"

"Far beyond the mountains," he pointed towards the south.

The land was flat as far as the eye could see. His words meant that this devil would be a very long way from here. I knew from my maps that the only high ground that could remotely be called mountains was far to the south, across the border in Guinea. Beyond the mountains must mean southern Guinea or even Liberia. It was several hundred miles from here. Could I justify the time to go into unknown territory in search of a sorcerer, to ask him to lift this strange curse? What would my masters in London think if they knew I was even considering it? They'd have me committed to an asylum for the insane.

"Is this Poro magic or Leopard Men?" I asked.

"We do not speak of such things," Etu looked uncomfortable, "But one of their sorcerers is needed to lift the curse."

Oh dear, this was beginning to look even more dubious. I wasn't sure I wanted to tangle with that sort of thing. Everything I had ever heard about Poro was evil. I had met cruel magic in other places, like the delta states of Nigeria, and in some of the Voodoo areas of Dahomey, even a few in Togo and Ghana; but they had all been minor league compared to the secretive Poro sect in Liberia and the Leopard Men of Sierra Leone.

This needed some serious consideration. I decided to sleep on it and try out the fruit in my oil extracting machine in the morning before deciding anything. I needed to be sure we could collect viable quantities of oil before committing to any venture like that.

I thanked Etu for his wisdom and went back to my Land Rover to prepare food.

EARLY THE NEXT MORNING I drove out to the stick hut, parking beside the old tree stump I had used as an anvil. I sat the machine on the tail gate, checked it was clean, and fitted a collecting jar beneath the spout. With the first basket of oranges to hand, I pulled back the spring clips and fitted an orange to the spindle. It took only a few moments to wind up the clockwork mechanism and release the spring.

The orange began to spin, slowly at first, but gathering speed before I lowered the arm with the needle and saw it start to scratch a fine groove in the skin of the spinning fruit. An immediate spurt of zest stung my eyes and I hastily closed the lid so that any more that was flung upwards would be retained.

It took fifteen seconds for the arm to traverse the orange. It dropped as it passed beyond the fruit. I stopped the motor and lifted the lid. Fine droplets of oil coated everything inside and the pungent aroma was strong. The fruit, formerly a glossy yellowish green, was now rough and fuzzy where the needle had scored its surface.

Albert had been clever when he constructed the machine: by moving a simple lever, you could make it run in reverse, carrying the arm back to its starting point. I replaced the fruit, started again and spent the next two hours changing the oranges and rewinding the motor until I had used everything in the first basket.

To begin with, there was only the fine mist of oil on the inside of the cover to show that anything had been extracted. As I proceeded, it became more obvious. After thirty oranges, the droplets had become big enough to begin dribbling down the glass into the jar below. This was most encouraging.

By the time I had a quarter of an inch of oil in the jar it was getting hot, so I moved the Land Rover a little closer to a thorn tree and spread a cotton sheet as a sunshade, tying one side to the vehicle and the other to the branches. The shade made the work much more comfortable.

By midday I had scraped more than five hundred oranges and there was a good quantity of oil in the jar. Among my vehicle spares I found and old windscreen wiper blade and cut a short piece off this to scrape the inside surfaces of the machine's cover to encourage the last drops of the oil down into the jar. If it took so much work to get this small amount, it would be wicked to waste even the smallest drop.

There was a large pile of orange scented debris where I had been working. It was beginning to bake in the sun and would soon begin fermenting. I wondered if the juice could be improved by fermentation and distillation and had visions of a double-barrelled cottage industry: orange oil and orange liqueur. One step at a time, I told myself.

22 ~ A French connection

TIME, IT SEEMED, WAS IN short supply. I was expected in Senegal in two weeks' time. Before that I had meetings in Bamako with the government's water authorities about a new borehole project we were planning between Gao, Kidal and In-Tebezas in the northern desert region. Somewhere along the way, I needed to go back to Anéhigouya to pick up my plane.

I had come by road this time as there had been a string of brief visits to make on the way here and few of those places had space to land the plane nearby. There was also no landing strip here yet, so before leaving, I resolved to clear a piece of ground so that next time I could fly in.

I went back to the village to consult.

Word had gone round about the fruit and everyone was curious, but opinions were divided. Some were deeply suspicious, saying it would be dangerous to take oranges from the trees because they were bewitched. Something evil was bound to happen. Such was the extent of their superstition that a few even suggested it was putting the whole community in jeopardy. Others, seeing potential for something new, were more enthusiastic and crowded round to look at my little bottle of oil. They wanted to touch the magic machine that had made it.

The little bottle, despite having a good tight screw cap, still smelled strongly of oranges and the liquid inside had an oily, viscous appearance with a greenish hue and microscopic bits of pith suspended in it. It would need to be filtered before I could offer a sample to anyone. A hospital centrifuge might solve this problem.

The village headman was one of the sceptics. He was worried that any interference with the orange trees might bring misfortune to his community, despite them being more than twelve miles from his village. Nasia agreed to talk to him to help convince him it would be all right. It seemed best to let her do this in her own way, so I took the Land Rover and went to look for a suitable piece of ground for an airstrip. It didn't take long to find a spot, a mile short of the stick hut. It had the benefit of being naturally clear of trees and fairly flat. Only a few small bushes, some clumps of heavy grass and one termite castle needed to be removed. On past record, the termite castle looked like being the hardest part as the one that had wrecked my sump had been like concrete. At least this one was out in the open, not under a vehicle.

After supper, I settled down for the night on top of the Land Rover. It was cooler up there and the slight breeze kept mosquitoes away so I slept well. In the morning, the headman approached and told me he would support my plan. He clearly still had doubts, but his about-face was spectacular. I hoped it would be possible to find a Western purchaser who would make the project viable so that his village really gained something from it.

When I asked for help to clear the piece of ground for an airstrip, he was again a little reluctant. Nasia had arrived by this time and said something to him which I didn't understand. He immediately went off and returned a few minutes later with five men armed with hoes and machetes. He had brought his own machete too, making it clear he was a part of this thing. He was going to share its glory or go down in a blaze if it failed. I began to like him.

We all piled into the Land Rover and went to clear the strip.

In less than two hours the job was done. Even the termite castle was a thing of the past. I promised the headman that next time I came I would take him up in my plane and let him view his village like the kites do, from high above. He looked dubious but said I would be welcome when I returned. With only a little persuasion, he agreed to store the oil machine in his own compound, and not to let anyone fiddle with it while I was gone.

The next morning I started back to Bamako for meetings before heading home to collect my aeroplane and fly myself to Senegal.

MY FIRST STOP IN SENEGAL was in Dakar, the capital, where life was a lot more sophisticated. The city centre was like Paris, with stately buildings, broad tree-lined boulevards and squares with gardens in them. Besides a well-equipped hospital, where I was able to get my little bottle of orange oil spun and filtered until its contents gleamed, there were branches of Parisian shops, some of which sold expensive perfumes. It didn't take long to get the addresses of half a dozen perfume houses which might be interested in my product. I spent a useful afternoon dividing my sample into little vials acquired from the hospital lab and writing letters to accompany them. As I flew north to visit the Senegal River projects, the samples were winging their way to Paris.

WHEN I RETURNED TO Dakar a week later, a telex had arrived from one of the Parisian *parfumiers*. It contained a long list of questions, most of which I didn't understand because I knew virtually nothing about the perfume trade. But there was a telephone number, so I booked a phone call and sent a telex warning Monsieur Lucien Dréfault of Parfums Fragigny to expect my call.

Later that afternoon, I spoke to M. Dréfault and it quickly became apparent that he was very interested. He decided it would be easier for him to send someone to discuss my proposal in situ and negotiate a deal. He would like his man to inspect the source and the production facility and meet the workforce. His colleague would have full authority to make an agreement.

I explained that the source was way out in the bush, the production facility at the moment consisted of one Heath Robinson contraption and there was no regular workforce, but this didn't deter him. I don't think he had the slightest idea what Mali was like. He told me his business partner, M. Marcel Dupuy, would come in three weeks' time.

I asked if M. Dupuy had ever been to Africa before.

"Africa? I thought your telex came from Dakar," he said, surprised.

"Yes, that's in Senegal, on the west coast of Africa,"

"No matter, I'll send him there, then."

"But the project is seven hundred miles away in the next country," I said.

"So where shall I send him?"

"Try Bamako. I'll pick him up from there and take him to the project area. He'll need to be prepared to go out in the bush. It's a bit primitive."

"Bamako, where's that?" he asked.

"In Mali."

"Is that near Perpignan?"

This man was unbelievable. I was tempted to tell him to drop the whole thing, but he seemed keen and willing to spend money. To me, this meant the oil really was worth something, so I hung on.

"No, it's in Africa. He'll need a passport and a visa from the Malian embassy in Paris to visit," I explained. "You make the arrangements and then send a telex to this number to confirm the details." I dictated the number of the PTT exchange in Ouahigouya that I used as my base for communications. "Give me at least two weeks' notice."

Before leaving I arranged for any more telexes arriving for me to be forwarded to Ouahigouya. In the event, only one other company did reply, but they had a secure supply of cultivated oil from a source in Morocco. At least they had the courtesy to respond. That's more than the other four did.

23 ~ Fresh scent

DESPITE HIS PARTNER'S SHAKY knowledge of geography, M. Marcel Dupuy duly arrived in Bamako; a model of Parisian chic, smelling like a lady of the night from Montmartre. The clothing in which he arrived was clearly *haute couture*. I hoped he had something more suitable for the bush. His luggage consisted of a matched pair of brand new Louis Vuitton leather suitcases with braided straps and shiny brass buckles. I wondered how they would look after a couple of weeks in the bush.

Since I had arrived in my plane, I had borrowed an old car from a friend to take him from the airport to his hotel. As I dropped him off he asked for my room number so that we might meet up and dine together. "I'm not staying here," I explained. "I'm staying in a small hotel down near the river."

"Then I will stay there too," he announced with Gallic gallantry. "We need to be together so you can tell me all about where you are getting the fragrance from."

"It's a bit basic," I protested. "And there's no air conditioning. You'll be more comfortable here, really. I'll come and take you out to dinner and we can talk then."

"I insist," he said and turned to the door, motioning the porter who had brought his cases in from the car to take them out again.

On your own head be it, I thought. Shrugging my regrets for his loss of custom to the hotel receptionist, I followed him out to the car.

The Hotel Lunaire, where I stayed when in Bamako, was a small place on the bank of the River Niger. Its facilities were basic and had seen better days; its glory was now no more than a distant memory. I used it because I knew the owner through one of his cousins, and it was a quiet, discrete place from which I could come and go without any fuss. The staff always made me welcome as if I were a family member. It was also within walking distance of an unprepossessing little restaurant that served the best fried frogs legs in town.

It was to this restaurant that I planned to take my guest for dinner. He would no doubt be disappointed with the wine list – they didn't have one – but he might get a cold beer and we'd be able to talk in peace for as long as we wanted.

I watched his face as we arrived at the hotel and thought I saw a flicker of disappointment, but it didn't last. Well, I had warned him, and he was in for far worse when we went out to the bush. I gave him half an hour to get settled in his room before we met on the hotel terrace overlooking the river. Terrace was perhaps a grand description: in reality it was no more than a clear patch of ground between the hotel building and the river bank. Two palm trees offered a little shade from the late sun but it was otherwise open. Two rickety garden tables and a few simple chairs were the only furniture. I chose the cleanest of these and asked Abdulla, the proprietor, if he could rustle up something to quench the thirst.

Fresh lime and soda? That would do fine.

When the drinks arrived, it was clear Abdulla had excelled himself. He presented us with frosted glasses and a large jug of freshly squeezed lime juice and soda. Better still, clinking in it were ice cubes that tumbled into the glasses as he poured.

The Frenchman was very intense. He lost no time in getting down to business with a flurry of questions. Most of them I couldn't answer, so I suggested it might be better for me to explain from the beginning how the project had started, and what actions I had taken. Tomorrow I would fly him to the area where the oranges grew and show him how the oil was extracted. We would stay in the village for a few nights to talk to the villagers about how to develop the enterprise. He could then consider whether it was viable for his company.

I was pinning a lot on this last point, for the villagers desperately needed the income the sale of the oil would bring. I hoped that when I learned more about his craft, and he understood what producing this product in the bush actually involved, we could formulate answers to most of his questions.

He was an attentive listener and got quite excited when I told him about my Eureka moment with the soap makers in Dogbo-Itémé. I retrieved a bar of the soap from my room to show him. He sniffed it and seemed impressed with the smell, even if the soap itself wasn't very good. He insisted I tell him more about that enterprise after we had dealt with the orange oil. His company might be interested in that as well. Things were looking positive.

As the sun sank into the river, we walked along to the restaurant and ordered our supper: frogs' legs and fried potatoes. When the food arrived, Marcel's eyes – he had by now insisted I should call him Marcel rather than M. Dupuy – stood out like chapel hat pegs. He exclaimed that he had never seen such huge frogs' legs and asked where they came from.

"From about twenty yards that way," I said, pointing into the gloom towards the murky waters flowing past our table. We could hear a chorus of other frogs croaking in the darkness. "The owner's little boy catches them fresh each afternoon."

"This is a land of surprises," he said and launched into another enquiry about the orange oil. Single-minded didn't come close to describing him. Today his intensity might have made me wonder if he had Asperger's Syndrome, but at the time I had never heard of it. If he noticed the lack of wine with the meal, he didn't mention it, making do with mineral water and, later, strong coffee.

24 ~ Essence of orange

A FEW WEEKS EARLIER, I had flown down to the west of the
Ivory Coast. My destination was the little town of Danane, where
I had a meeting with the warden of the Nimba Wildlife Reserve.
He had heard about work I had done in the Northern Game
Reserve in Ghana, and wanted me to help him with provision of
consistent water supplies for the animals in his reserve.

Had I known there was an airstrip at the reserve, I could have
gone directly to the park, but the warden took advantage of my
visit to make a rare trip to town. It turned out well because when,
over lunch, I told him I wanted to find a devil to lift the curse from
the orange trees in Mali, he roared with laughter and said he knew
just the man. Devils were not confined to Liberia: there were
plenty to be found in the villages around his reserve. It was close
to the border and for operational matters it worked jointly with
another reserve across the frontier in Liberia.

Leaving his truck in Danane, we flew up to the game park and
were able to inspect the areas where he needed water from the air.
In half an hour, we had identified a number of locations where
small barrages and storage tanks could be created without using

sophisticated equipment, and I was able to offer the kind of advice that might have taken several weeks if I'd made a ground visit.

After we had viewed all his locations, we landed on the reserve's airstrip and he sent a ranger to summon a local devil. We settled down in his headquarters building and while we awaited the arrival of this worthy, I drew basic plans and sketches to show him how to build storage tanks in the narrow upland valleys.

Before dark, the devil appeared – or rather didn't appear. A strange figure approached, swathed in heavy raffia skirts and an all-enveloping dark green top. Its head was hidden behind a gruesome mask with raffia hair and beard, a huge hat, and on its hands it wore enormous floppy gloves. It looked like a Womble in drag.

From the way it moved, there was clearly a human inside this extraordinary costume, but none of him, not even a minute part, could be seen. There was no way of knowing either the gender or the age of the person within. Even when it spoke, for speak it did, the voice was androgynous. It was a clear, light voice, but probably not a young one. There was another surprise when the apparition spoke, for it spoke English, with an American accent.

Perhaps I shouldn't have been surprised since Liberia had been created by slaves freed from the Americas and sent back to Africa to carve a homeland where their forebears came from. Or at least, somewhere near there. So many had returned in the last century they had largely displaced the Creole tribes and their languages. American English was now the primary national language.

The devil listened to the head warden as he explained that I had come a long way and needed a curse lifted. Then it turned to me and demanded imperiously that I explain. Every so often as I talked, and for no obvious reason, the creature would spin on the spot, stopping suddenly with a rustle of its grass skirts. The first time it did this I stopped speaking and it squawked at me, "Talk! Talk! Don't stop!"

So I carried on speaking, trying to ignore its gyrations.

I had brought a small vial of the orange oil with me and I placed this on the ground in front of the devil when I started explaining. After one of the twirls, it stooped and picked up the vial, thrusting in deep inside a fold of its green upper garment before resuming its gyrations.

When I finished explaining, there was a long pause and the devil appeared to squat, reducing itself to half its height. It looked like a deflated scarecrow, sitting on a pile of straw.

We waited.

It shuffled several times but said nothing. The head warden whispered in my ear that it was divining. He had seen a lot of this sort of thing before. We should wait. It could take some time.

We sat and waited for almost an hour before the devil suddenly roared, rising to its full height, spinning round and round, arms spread wide. It stopped as suddenly as it had begun and announced that it would cost fifty dollars to lift the curse, payable in cash. Now. Its hands were held out in front, ready to receive the money.

I asked if it would accept CFA francs, which were all I had with me.

"Dollars! Only dollars!" it roared.

I had a small supply of foreign currency in the aeroplane so I explained that I would have to go and get dollars.

Without a word the devil squatted again. I took this as consent for me to leave and borrowed a bicycle from outside the warden's office to ride the half-mile to the airstrip where I had left a small boy guarding my plane. There was a small compartment in the

The devil appeared to squat... it looked like a deflated scarecrow, sitting on a pile of straw. (Photo courtesy of Tim Butcher)

roof of the cabin in which I kept important documents relating to the plane. These included a little currency, among which were some twenty dollar bills. I took these and returned to find the warden still sitting and the devil still crouched, exactly as I had left them.

Returning to my seat, I held up three banknotes. A man in a grass skirt who had accompanied the devil took the money from my hand. He looked at the banknotes, nodded and walked back to stand behind the devil, handing the banknotes to a man in a white smock. He was obviously the devil's treasurer.

The devil remained immobile. We waited. Eventually it rose, slowly this time and turned leisurely on the spot, in the opposite direction to the way it had spun so energetically before. It made two complete rotations that could have been steps in a stately gavotte, and then announced that the curse would be lifted. It would come again at dawn and bring me an amulet for the orange trees. The amulet would release the spirits.

This was a very different kind of magic from any I had encountered before. Or was it all just hocus-pocus, smoke and mirrors for the gullible? I was accustomed to sorcerers who chanted and mumbled; ones who threw bones, banged drums or struck iron bells; sorcerers who caused spirits to whirl in the air and who put substance into their magic. During this business I had felt nothing. The air hadn't tingled, nothing had caressed the nape of my neck with silky fingers, there had been no smells, no energy flowing around us; simply this strange figure whirling and squatting. I felt a bit of a fool and indicated as much to the head warden.

"Don't worry," he reassured me. "If it says it has lifted the curse, be sure it has done so. I hope you have more money. It will cost you another fifty dollars when it brings you the amulet tomorrow."

"He took sixty from me just now," I remarked, slightly peeved that I hadn't had any ten dollar bills.

"Then it'll probably take the same again tomorrow. Be grateful the devil was able to remove the curse."

Clearly the head warden was a believer who understood this sort of magic. Well he should; he lived with it in his back yard. Since he had been very professional in all our other dealings, perhaps it would be as well for me to respect his opinion and believe the curse had been lifted.

Since I now had to remain here until the devil returned in the morning, I borrowed the bicycle again, returned to the aircraft and erected my anti-goat fence, turning on the electric fencing unit as I left it. I stayed overnight at the ranger station and made a little model to show the rangers how to build the kind of storage tanks that would help solve their water supply problem.

As he had promised, the devil appeared at dawn and demanded fifty dollars for the amulet. Again I held up three twenties and his henchman came forward. He took the money, counted it and then returned one bill to me. "Fifty dollars," he said. "You already gave sixty."

That surprised me and made me think this fellow might be an honest sorcerer. If so, it was a rare bird, I thought. Perhaps I should accept that it's done what it had said.

Again the devil stood silent. Time began to crawl until a small brown arm of childish proportions emerged from the front of the raffia skirt. The hand held an amulet.

I went forward and took this and the hand hastily withdrew. Was there a child under there? I wondered, or was this a magical manifestation? It was best not to question it. Accept the amulet in good faith, and consider the deal done, I decided.

The devil stood for a few minutes more and then, without a word, gave a quick twirl and floated off, disappearing behind a building.

Later that morning, I flew the head warden back to Danane to recover his truck. We said goodbye, both satisfied that this had been a worthwhile encounter and I promised to visit again in three months' time to see how he was getting on. I gave him my radio frequency to call if he needed further advice.

As I took off, I wondered what the devil had done with the vial of orange oil it had secreted in its clothing. I lifted the amulet to my nose and found it had a distinct whiff of orange essence about it. Did that answer my question? There might be more than met the eye in this unfamiliar brand of magic.

25 ~ Expert in the orchards

AFTER AN EARLY BREAKFAST, Marcel and I drove to the airport. We went to the light aircraft park this time, where my plane was waiting, fully fuelled and ready to go. It was a bit of a struggle getting his two smart suitcases into the back as my Mobylette was already in there and we would need to use it when we arrived. There was also a can of spare fuel and a box of other essentials I had promised the headman I would bring. Marcel's cases weren't particularly heavy, but they were bulky. I wondered what exotic Parisian fashions he had brought to wear in the bush.

Marcel took everything as it came, made no fuss whatsoever and was so wrapped up in his own trade and what we were going to see that he was oblivious to the contrasts between here and his usual environment in Paris. He'd never been in a light aircraft before, he told me; they don't have many in the 17th Arrondissement, but he adapted to it as if he were merely getting into a taxi in the rue des Batignolles. He hadn't complained about the accommodation in the Hotel Lunaire, and didn't mind there being no wine with his meal, although he clearly knew a lot about the stuff and enjoyed it at home. To top it all, he was not the least interested in the different scenes, sounds and smells of life around him. I wondered how he was going to react when faced with Etu in the village.

I hadn't yet told him about the complication of the curse on the orange trees, but if he ran true to form, that wouldn't be a problem. I hadn't been back to the village since my encounter with the devil and its amulet was here with us in the plane.

It took just over an hour to fly to the area and a further fifteen minutes to locate my new airstrip. It was some weeks since it had been cleared and I hoped it had remained that way and that no termites had built a new castle in the middle of the landing ground. We were now between the rainy seasons, but the ground was still fresh and small plants grew fast, so a lot could have changed. Luck was with us. The strip was still clear and, to my complete surprise, there was someone waiting beside it with a small fire burning. As we circled he piled leaves onto the blaze and made smoke, showing me the wind direction.

The figure by the fire turned out to be Akleno, who told me his mother had foreseen our arrival and told him to go and wait for us. She told him to light the fire and make smoke when the big bird was above him. This was amazing; I knew that Nasia had never seen an aeroplane and couldn't possibly know that the wind direction might be important. I thanked Akleno as he helped me unload the supplies we had brought for the village. When he saw Marcel's cases, he said there was too much to carry. Someone would come back later with a donkey cart to collect the cases.

We erected my anti-goat fence around the plane, put covers over the windscreen and engine ports and headed towards the village on foot. It was nearly an hour's walk but it gave me an opportunity to quiz Akleno and hear what had been going on in the village. After his initial hostility when I had first returned Nasia and Ayenu, he was now remarkably pleased to have them around again. He valued his mother's ability as a seer, and I guessed she had told him things that caused his change of heart as he was now very friendly and willing to assist me in any way he could.

Marcel declined his offer of a cart to bring his suitcases to the village, saying he had everything he needed until the morning in the small bag he carried. In any case, one valise contained equipment we would only need at the orange orchards, two of which we had flown over on our way in, to give Marcel sight of the trees and the spread of their locations. It would be more useful to have help carrying the case there in the morning.

The headman greeted us courteously but he was still a little reserved. Akleno told me he was afraid of so many foreigners coming to his village, and worried about what might be upset as a result. I tried to reassure him that Marcel was only going to be here a few days. There wouldn't be a train of other foreigners following, although if this project took off, one or two others might need to make brief visits. He accepted this, but still looked very dubious.

As he had in Bamako, Marcel made himself at home in the spartan accommodation the village offered. Someone in Paris had advised him to bring a mosquito net. At dusk he hung this from the rafters of the hut we were given, and settled down on the grass sleeping mat as though it was normal.

This man was still a bit of a closed book. He gave away very little about himself. He wasn't being secretive; it just seemed there wasn't much there to give away. He was so wrapped up in his profession that nothing else mattered. Anything not closely related to perfume wasn't relevant to him. Even so, I was surprised that having spent all his life in Paris he wasn't the least bit curious about the culture and lives of the people he now found himself among. The only comment he offered was when we were offered some village beer, brewed from sorghum. He swallowed a good mouthful and said, "I don't think I'll be recommending this to my wine merchant." Then he carried on drinking.

WE WERE UP EARLY and on our way to the aeroplane soon after dawn, with a comet's tail of curious villagers and a flock of chattering children in our wake. Everything was as we had left it. Once the anti-goat fence was deactivated, Marcel removed the smaller of his two valises and laid it on the ground. I was curious to see what it contained and completely unprepared for the sight when he opened the lid.

The inside was fitted with padded compartments, each containing a little bottle. Half of these contained liquid of varying hues. These, Marcel told me, were scent control samples. Lifting out the top tray revealed larger items underneath, including a small manually operated centrifuge. It was operated with a crank handle like an old wind-up gramophone and was capable of spinning four little vials at dizzying speeds, fast enough to make them disappear into a circular blur. A set of balance scales, various glass sampling dishes, a collection of strange looking instruments like a school dissection kit, and a small optical microscope occupied the other spaces. In pockets in the lid were books of tables and colour charts and a notebook for records. It was a mobile laboratory in a suitcase. My estimation of Marcel's professionalism and dedication rose several notches. I assumed he knew how to use all this kit.

He checked that everything was in order, closed the lid, and declared himself ready to go and look at the orange trees. They were a few miles from the airstrip so one of the villagers obligingly hoisted Marcel's valise onto his head and we set off with Akleno leading the way.

We had not gone far before I became aware of another presence walking slightly behind me. It was Etu, the sorcerer, who said he wanted to be there when I hung the devil's amulet in the trees. He had to assure himself that the curse was indeed lifted; the headman had asked him to check that I was telling them the truth.

Evidently I had been right about the headman who, even though Nasia had told him this would work out all right, was still sceptical about everything I proposed or told him.

Etu was interested in my visit to the devil. He had asked many questions when I told him about it the previous evening. Now he wanted to go over it again, probing to understand the nature of the curse. He was particularly interested in why that particular devil might think he had the power to lift the curse, because it had been imposed so long ago, and the devil was so far away from the trees.

Scepticism wasn't just the purview of the headman.

We talked through it all again and when I showed him the amulet, he examined it in detail, turning it over in his hands, feeling to see if any spiritual essence would reveal itself.

"Will this only let you use the fruit for the oil, or will it make the fruit sweet?" he asked.

"I don't know. I didn't think to ask that."

"Is there a ritual to make it active?"

"I don't think so. The devil just told me to hang it in the trees."

"Maybe I should call the spirits to witness when you do this."

"Won't they see anyway?"

"It would be better to tell them what you are doing. Spirits don't like to be taken for granted."

He had a point. "You call the spirits and tell me when to hang the amulet in the tree," I said.

"You will know. The spirits will tell you," he said, thrusting the amulet back into my hands and moving slightly aside to start preparing his mind.

Etu began to call the spirits as soon as we reached the first grove. Those villagers who came with us clustered round to listen and watch. Children hushed their chatter and slid in to stand close among the adults' legs, aware that something important was happening, but wary because it involved the sorcerer, who inspired awe and trepidation in the young. Not just the young; some of the adults looked a bit wary too.

Etu's words rose from a mumble to a chant and I could hear the varying tones. Before long the first forms fluttering in the air appeared, skipping through the branches and buzzing round above our heads. Silky fingers danced lightly down my back and something began tugging at the amulet hanging round my neck on a leather thong. The feeling was so strong it made me look down, but I couldn't see anything.

Etu turned round, took my hand and placed it over the amulet. "Hold it," he said, and resumed communing with the spirits. I could feel the amulet vibrating under my fingers, and getting warm, as if it had energy of its own.

Etu's tone changed. He had called the spirits and was now explaining why we were here. How I knew this I'm not sure, but it felt right.

The amulet began to pulse and I could feel its throbbing against my chest.

Suddenly, the tugging at the amulet stopped, even though Etu's words continued for some minutes. Then there was quiet. Nothing moved, nothing fluttered; the fizz that had permeated the atmosphere earlier was gone. I looked round to see how Marcel was responding and found he wasn't there. One of the children pointed and I saw him some distance away, walking among the trees and looking up into the branches. He stopped now and then to sniff at a flower, to touch a leaf and rub it between his fingers, and then moved on. Oblivious to what had been happening and not understanding the necessity for the delay, he had sauntered off to do what he did understand. I hoped the spirits wouldn't find his behaviour disrespectful.

I felt a strong impulse to go in among the trees myself and hang the amulet on one of them. For some reason I knew it would be wrong to hang it on the nearest tree. As if being guided, I walked among them, touching trees as I passed until a hot tingling in my fingertips told me this was the one.

Snatching my hand away, I inspected my fingers expecting to see them covered with fire ants. These small demons love citrus trees and live in symbiosis with them. But there was nothing to see and no fire ants.

This tree was waiting for the amulet.

I lifted it from my neck, held the amulet aloft for the villagers to see and wound the thong round a branch, knotting it to make sure it wouldn't slip and fall off. After a glance at Etu, to see that he was satisfied with my action, I went after Marcel to see what he wanted to do next.

Marcel was collecting blossoms, two or three from each tree he passed, together with a few leaves from the same tree and a single fruit. When he had enough he returned to where his mobile laboratory had been deposited and began opening vials and comparing aromas with the scent from the flowers.

His actions made no sense to me as all the flowers smelled the same, but to his trained nose, they were different. As he finished with each one, he laid it on the corresponding leaves in a neat grid on the open lid of the case. After sniffing all the flowers, he repeated the procedure with the fruits, scraping the surface of each with a blade and sniffing the zest, comparing this with another set of scented vials from his case.

It was fascinating to watch. His total absorption in the task meant he was oblivious to the villagers who were now wandering among the trees, picking flowers to put in their hair and looking longingly at the fruit. There was little fruit in their diet and if these oranges had been edible they would have made a valuable addition.

Marcel had taken twenty different samples. When the flowers and the oranges had all been sniffed, he produced a bundle of coloured threads and walked back among the trees, trying a thread to each tree. He used six colours and when I asked what it was all about, he told me they represented six different scents. If they could be separated, they would produce very different oils. This meant processing fruit only from trees with the same coloured thread in any one batch. Once one colour had been processed, the machine would have to be cleaned before oranges from trees with a different coloured thread were done, and so on.

"Does this really matter?" I asked.

"But of course! Purity is important. That 's what makes a great perfume."

You live and learn, I thought.

26 ~ Growing enterprise

WE SPENT THE REST OF the day in the first orange grove. By the time we left, Marcel had tied a coloured thread to every tree. Although he had identified six different perfume groups, most of the trees bore either blue or yellow threads. We brought two baskets of fruit from each colour to the village. Marcel wanted to spend the following morning processing these and testing the results in his little laboratory. First we had to make sure the machine was absolutely clean after the last time it had been used.

When the machine was brought out in the morning, Marcel behaved as if he was completely familiar with it and how it worked, despite never having seen anything like it before. I asked how the oil he normally used was collected. By suction, he told me, so this method was new to him. I marvelled at his adaptability as he instructed how the machine should be cleaned. From a little jar of crystals, he dropped a small scoopful into a water container, asking for all the machine's surfaces to be washed thoroughly with this and then dried in the sun for an hour. The sunlight would help sterilise it. When the machine was clean, we began processing the blue thread oranges.

Seeing the oil extractor in action and hearing the whirring of its clockwork motor, caused a lot of interest among the villagers. They love mechanical things, and the aroma it produced added to the excitement. After the first few oranges had been processed and Marcel had tried his hand at operating it, some of the villagers had a go. They would need to be able to do this if the project was to work, so they might as well start learning from the beginning.

Akleno was one of the first to try. He proved to have very dextrous fingers, even though his thumbs were callused, and had no trouble in operating it. I asked him about his thumbs; he told me it was from playing his kora. That evening, he promised us, he would bring out his instrument and play for us.

Callused thumbs: the mark of a kora player.

Meanwhile there were oranges to spin and he was enjoying the task. Several other villagers proved to be quite dextrous and it was simple enough for them all to learn how to make the machine work. This augured well, for I realised that if Marcel used the same colour coding at the other orchards, we would need to have separate machines processing each colour of oranges. While each machine would still need cleaning at the end of each day, it would avoid cross-contamination. We might not be able to smell the difference, but Marcel certainly could, and he was the customer.

When I suggested multiple machines to Marcel, he agreed and asked how much they cost. I explained it was a one-off, made by the engineer who serviced my plane. When I told him how much I had paid for it, he merely nodded. He was willing to pay twice that sum for each machine as an up-front capital cost, and would sort out the details before he returned to Paris.

His willingness to throw money at the project was a most un-French attitude. He was behaving like an American! He had said nothing about exclusivity, but I felt sure he would require it.

By mid-morning, we had processed all the oranges from the first blue batch. From about eight hundred oranges, the contents of nine baskets, we obtained nearly 150 millilitres – a quarter of a pint – of oil. Marcel produced a supply of small vials and his balance. After a bit of fiddling and careful decanting, he marked a level on one vial by wrapping a sticky label round it. The other vials were to be filled level with the bottom of the label.

He showed the villagers once how to do this and stood back, letting them get on with it. A man called Musa displayed a talent for the task, so was appointed the bottle filler by popular vote.

In the afternoon, we collected more oranges from the blue trees. Processing continued until dusk and by then almost half a litre – three-quarters of a pint – of oil had been saved in a whole box of collection vials. The pile of exhausted fruit formed a mound over a yard high and was beginning to smell very fruity. No longer protected by its waterproof skin, the ripe fruit had started to ferment in the heat. Teams of children, always eager to get involved, were organised to pile the used fruit into baskets and carry it away from the village, dropping it in the bush in areas not frequented by the villagers. A big bag of boiled sweets turned this into a competition and before long the pile was cleared and every child in the village had earned a handful of sweets.

We decided to move the machine nearer to the trees the following day and do the work there. It made little sense carrying the fruit all the way to the village just to carry it off again and dump it in the bush. Oranges had been falling to the ground and rotting where they grew for many years. The only difference now was that they would pass through an intermediate stage by having the oil collected from their skin before landing on the ground.

A team of men set off at dawn to carry the machine to the orchard. It wasn't heavy, but it was an awkward load. Marcel and I followed a little later, stopping at the plane to pull out my Mobylette. I hadn't used it for a few days so it took a few yards of hard pedalling to start it, but in a few minutes it was puttering along with me driving and Marcel perched on the baggage rack behind. He seemed sublimely unaware of the discomfort of his position.

HARVESTING AND PROCESSING continued at the first grove, supervised by Akleno. Marcel and I used the Mobylette to explore the other stands of trees. These, in groups of several hundred trees, stretched in a curved line for almost six miles. He brought a supply of coloured cords with him and we marked trees for later use. One grove of three hundred trees used entirely yellow cords. Marcel said it was a good thing as these trees produced the strongest smelling oil. I made a note to tell Akleno to ensure the yellow fruit was worked next and be sure none of it was wasted. If the smell was stronger, it might make the oil worth a little more. We had yet to get round to discussing the economics of this operation; I knew it was something Marcel was considering carefully.

By the second evening, we had bottled another half litre of oil and Marcel was running out of vials. He had come well prepared but hadn't expected such abundance. He was careful to see that the remaining bottles were filled with representative samples from all the other coloured trees so they could be properly evaluated and compared when he got back to his perfumery in Paris.

That evening, we cleaned the machine for the final time and carried it back to be stored in Akleno's hut. Akleno had become the principal player in the village team. Although many other people had contributed to the work, he stood out from the crowd, speaking enough French and having adapted so quickly to the mechanical operation. He was a natural leader, so it made sense for him to be the villagers' representative when it came to negotiating. The headman would still be asked to give his approval, of course, and it was likely that the sorcerer would want to have his say. But Marcel was already treating Akleno as the de facto village head of the project.

Marcel produced a small jar of honey from his suitcase and mixed some with a few drops of orange oil. The change in scent was remarkable and obvious even to my unsophisticated nose. I asked Akleno if the villagers collected honey and he assured me they did whenever they found a wild hive but there were not many bees to be found in the part of the bush they used. Honey was a luxury.

"But there must be swarms with hives among the orange trees," I said. "Can't you find those and use that honey?"

"Not before. Nobody would go there. Maybe now, if the curse is lifted," he said.

I had forgotten that the villagers never went near the trees before my visit to the devil. Etu had expressed himself satisfied, as much as any sorcerer ever does, and the spirits had allowed us to harvest a generous amount of oil. The evidence suggested the curse was now well and truly lifted. That being so, and as there were still lots of bees among the trees, there was no reason why the villagers couldn't farm them and share their honey. If it was any good, Marcel might buy that too.

I spoke quietly to Akleno and he agreed to send men in the morning to look for a wild beehive among the orange trees. If they succeeded, they would bring some honey for Marcel to test. We could start by asking the village basket weavers to make a skep in the morning, and try to tempt the bees into using it. I hoped smearing a little of Marcel's honey on the inside of the basket and placing it in the trees might be enough to get the wild bees to take over. Time would tell.

During the next three days, by making forays on my Mobylette, Marcel and I managed to visit and colour code seven different orchards within a day's good walk of the village. Some were small patches with only a few dozen trees, but they bore fruit nonetheless. Three orchards had over five hundred trees in them, so their potential was good.

There was never any hard evidence that the existence of a curse on the orange trees was more than hearsay, despite the sorcerer's affirmation that there were troubled spirits present. But superstition had been strong and the bitterness of the fruit remained an unexplained anomaly. After three days working among the trees, the villagers seemed satisfied that the curse had gone. Now I hoped there would be nothing to stop them going among the trees and exploiting them in all sorts of ways. They were too good a resource to ignore in their marginal economy.

Producing honey as well as oil sounded like a good start to me.

I decided to take some oranges and soil samples to a proper agricultural research laboratory to see if anything could be done to improve the flavour of the fruit and make it usable. If the trees could be persuaded to grow more palatable oranges, there might be the potential for marmalade production here as well as orange oil. Elephant grass grew commonly in the region; there were big stands of it nearby. If that grew well, there was no reason why sugar cane shouldn't grow equally well, yet nobody cultivated it here. The two plants are both species of grass, after all. With sugar and fruit available, marmalade manufacture ought to be possible. I was due to go to Togo in a few weeks time, so I would make a side visit to the Franciscan monastery at Dzogbegan and ask the advice of the monks there. They had established a thriving jam industry, using forest fruits, the produce from their own orchards, and locally grown sugar cane.

After we had eaten on the fifth evening, I asked Marcel what he thought of the project. He had proved the supply of usable oils here, now it was time to declare his level of interest. Did he want to buy the stuff for his company, or should I look elsewhere?

27 ~ Economics

THE SUGGESTION THAT I might ask another perfume house produced an immediate look of horror on Marcel's face. "No, no, no, you must not tell anyone else about this oil. I will buy it and give a fair price," he spluttered.

I looked at him quizzically, expecting more, but he hesitated. I could almost hear the cogs whirring inside his head as he decided what he should offer. Then it all came tumbling out.

"High quality oil could be worth as much as 2,500 francs a litre," he blurted, stumbling over his words in his haste to get them out. He obviously felt more comfortable talking about perfume than money.

My mind started computing.

"Is that French francs, CFA, or Malian francs?" I asked.

"Why, French francs, of course." His vehemence made me think he had been going to follow this statement by asking if there were any other kind of francs. How stupid of me; of course he could only think in metropolitan terms.

I smiled. French francs were worth much more than CFA or Malian francs.

After a moment, he went on to say that he would like me to arrange for two additional machines to be made as soon as possible. He would pay the going rate for them and loan them to the project for as long as the villagers continued working and supplying his company. He would also buy the present machine for what it had cost.

Based on the amount of oil we had extracted in the time he had been here and the number of trees he had surveyed, he estimated it should be possible to produce between one and a half and two litres a month. He wanted to buy ten litres per year and would pay the packing and shipping costs for this to be flown from Bamako to Paris. The villagers would be responsible for getting it to Bamako, but without refrigeration the oil needed to be no more than four weeks old when shipped. Records must be kept to confirm this because, as he explained, the oil could go stale and lose its aroma if it was too old. Since there was no way of keeping it cool, it must be fresh.

"Oh, it can be kept cool," I said. "What temperature does it need?"

"Cold, but you do not have a frigidaire," he protested.

"Would keeping butter solid in this heat convince you?"

"You can do that?"

"Of course."

I turned to Akleno and asked if he could get a litre of fresh goat's milk. We had brought mineral water in plastic bottles; he could use one of those. He went off to get the milk.

I turned back to Marcel and told him he would have solid butter by morning. He looked doubtful.

"What about the honey?" I asked. "I'm sure the villagers will collect some. Is that worth anything to you?"

He said he would need to see and test it before answering that and we agreed to make a concerted effort in the morning to find a wild beehive. If the skep idea worked, it could soon become much more organised, but proper equipment would be needed for extracting the honey and cleaning it. Wild honey usually contains a lot of twigs, wax and other impurities, which didn't matter so much if it was only going to be eaten by its collectors, but would severely reduce its value to a Parisian perfumier.

I agreed to look into this after Marcel had returned to Paris.

We had hardly completed this discussion when Akleno returned with a bottle of milk. I showed him how to shake it and asked for it to be shaken like this for a long time, until the fat globules separated from the milk and stuck to the inside of the bottle. Could he organise relays of youngsters to do this?

"If you have more sweets, they will do anything," he announced with a grin. I handed over more sweets, confident we would soon have some butter.

At this moment a group of men arrived with great excitement. They had found a wild beehive and managed to obtain a large chunk of the honeycomb. They looked slightly guilty as they explained that the honeycomb was no longer as big as when they had found it. All the way back from the orange grove their fingers had been probing to make sure there was honey inside and, of course, they had had to lick them clean, because they became so sticky. Even so, they dumped a huge lump of honeycomb on the ground. It was crawling with disturbed bees and, even in the half light, we could see other insects buzzing around it. All five men had been stung many times each – and the sting of the wild African bee is much more painful than the European bee – but their prize was worth the discomfort.

Marcel took several samples and spun them in his little centrifuge, separating the heavy solids and decanting the liquid honey into a clean container. He repeated this several times until he had the amount he wanted and then said the villagers should take the rest away. He was nervous about being stung by the bees and other bugs still attracted to it. The men went off with great glee to divide and consume their trophy.

By candle light, Marcel set about testing the honey. It was fascinating to watch him as he performed his alchemy. Eventually he expressed satisfaction with the quality and stated a price he was willing to pay. It sounded fair, but then anything was probably fair as, at present, nobody in the village had any cash income at all. Anything that earned them money was worth a great deal, even if the price was low. The honey was worth far less than the orange oil, of course, but that was to be expected.

Later Akleno returned with the plastic bottle of milk. Butter droplets had accumulated on the inside of the plastic. They had coalesced into a lump of white fat about the size of a walnut. The remaining liquid had become thin and translucent. We decanted the liquid, poured in more milk and asked the youngsters to shake it again, handing out sweets to those who had helped so far. In another hour they returned. The lump of butter was much bigger and the fluid was again thin and watery. This was enough butter to prove the point. I showed it to Marcel. He poked it with a finger and found it very soft. He put his finger in his mouth and agreed that it was butter, but it needed to be cool and solid or it would soon go rancid.

In the pannier on the back of my Mobylette there was a square of hessian sacking. I soaked this in water. Cutting the bottom off the plastic bottle made a dish. I scraped all the butter into this, wrapped it in shiny leaves from a bush outside and folded the hessian round the outside. I hung the strange package from a rafter under the eaves of our hut with the remainder of the bottle inverted, filled with water and hung above it. The bottle cap was slightly unscrewed so that it dripped slowly. Drops of water falling on the hessian would keep it moist while the evening breeze blowing though made it dry out. The continuous evaporation caused the whole thing to cool. It was sufficient for the butter to solidify by morning. I hoped it would convince Marcel that the villagers could keep his precious orange oil chilled so it could be shipped in prime condition.

After topping up the water bottle, we turned in, I with all my fingers crossed for a good result in the morning.

Dawn brought a fresh breeze and bright sunlight. I expected my evaporator to have dried up but Akleno had understood what I was doing and, realising the outcome could be important, had got up several times during the night to top up the water. The result was spectacular. Even Marcel, doubting Marcel, had to admit that the butter inside was not just firm, but cold enough to be truly solid.

"Is this cold enough for the orange oil?"

"If you can keep it cold like this," he said, "it will keep for at least two months."

28 ~ Sweetness of honey

BY MIDDAY, MARCEL HAD seen all he wanted to see. Now he needed to get back to Paris and work out whether he could make worthwhile perfume out of this oil. He repacked his mobile laboratory and a villager set off to the aeroplane, carrying it on his head. Marcel and I went round the village saying our goodbyes. I saved a special visit to last and went alone to see Nasia and Ayenu.

They were pleased to see me but were sad I was leaving again so soon. Nasia said she looked forward to seeing me on my next visit and I took this to mean she had foreseen that she would still be here. With anyone this old, life could be precarious, particularly here in the bush with no nearby medical services.

As I walked away it occurred to me that Ayenu's manner, while no less hospitable, had been slightly different. I wondered if it suggested he didn't expect to see me again.

We loaded the Mobylette into the aeroplane and piled Marcel's cases in on top of it. A small basket of oranges with more soil samples for the agricultural research station was crammed in and then we were off.

We flew over the nearest orange grove to let Marcel have one

Marcel Dupuy discusses colour-coding the trees with a villager.

last look at it and saw a lone figure standing facing the trees, his arms raised. Etu was performing another ritual. I wondered what this one was for and why he felt it was necessary. It was frustrating not knowing and even though I knew there was nothing I could do about it, small doubts niggled at my mind all the way back to Bamako.

Marcel stayed only one night in Bamako and the next day he took the afternoon flight to Paris. He promised to be in touch soon with a decision about whether his company would buy the orange oil.

Left on my own, I suddenly felt flat and purposeless after all the excitement, even though there was still plenty to do to make this project viable. I wandered round the market for a while and came across a woman selling honey in jars. The golden liquid caught my attention and I wanted to know where it came from, thinking there might already be a local source. It was disappointing to discover it had been imported from France, and she wanted an exorbitant price for it. I didn't buy any.

The next day, I flew to Bobo-Dioulasso to see Albert Daggia and tell him how his machine had worked in the field. I also wanted to ask him to make two more. He was delighted the first one had worked so well, but suggested future machines should be hand-operated rather than clockwork. If anything went wrong with the mechanism, it might be impossible to get it mended in the bush. A hand-operated machine would be simpler to make and ought to be within the competence of a village blacksmith to maintain. This got me thinking, I had not seen any sign of a blacksmith in Nasia's village. The only person with any mechanical flair was Akleno and a lot was already riding on him. This might be asking a bit much.

Over a meal, Albert and I fell to talking about the rest of the project. Since my first approach, he had become very interested and wanted to know about a lot of things an aero engineer would never normally take any interest in. My crazy project appealed to his sense of adventure. He wanted to go and visit once things got going properly. Of course he would assist with the oil extracting machines in any way possible.

When I mentioned the possibility of honey, he told me there was some honey production equipment lying idle in a store on the other side of the airport. He had found it some months earlier, when scouting the old workshops and sheds for spare parts. As far as he knew, it was still there. This could be very useful if a honey industry did develop. We went to have a look in the morning and found a mangle for rolling out sheets of beeswax to make comb frames for the hive, a lot of blank frames ready for wax and, best of all, a centrifuge for extracting the honey from framed combs.

There were also twenty-three simple wooden box hives. Enquiries revealed that the equipment had been brought in by a

Frenchman some years earlier to start honey production among the local farmers. Unfortunately he had died of malaria before the enterprise got under way. Albert offered to consult the airport manager and find out if we could buy the equipment.

TWO DAYS LATER, I WAS back in Anéhigouya telling my friend the Wa-Wa man all about what I had been up to. His guidance had proved useful when I went to seek the devil in Danane and once more his questioning steered my thinking into constructive channels. The mention of honey, and my doubts about getting people to manage the bees effectively, made him laugh. "Get an expert," he said, and with those three simple words changed my whole thinking about the project.

He pointed out that I had taken Oyadé from this village to help me with the well school in Mali. Why not do something similar for the honey?

"There is nobody here who keeps bees or who knows anything about them," I protested.

"You told me of beekeepers in Senegal," he said. "Isn't there someone there to help you in Mali?"

Why didn't I think of that? I had completely forgotten the farmers in Casamance who were producing good volumes of excellent quality honey. They even exported it to France. Some of those farmers had been dealing with bees for years. My only involvement had been to help them get modern equipment and to learn how to make simple hives from local resources. I had also helped them get access to commercial outlets. They could now return the favour and help get this project off the ground. I was due back in Senegal in three weeks' time; I would make a diversion to the south and consult the beekeepers co-operative.

Two weeks later, I flew to Bobo-Dioulasso and collected some of the equipment Albert had found. He had located the owners and persuaded them to sell it cheaply, so I reimbursed him from my discretionary fund. We managed to get half of the hives, with frames already waxed inside them, into the back of the aeroplane. This, together with my Mobylette, completely filled the space in the back and brought the aircraft's weight up to the limit I would want to fly with, given that I needed a full fuel load for the onward trip to Senegal. Another trip, or a visit by road, would be necessary to take the centrifuge and the wax mangle down there.

Albert was now keen to get involved so it might be a good idea to go by road and take him to visit. It could be useful to have someone else involved, particularly if the orange oil project took off, and he had made the harvesting machines, so their maintenance could be assured.

In the event, it was not difficult to find a beekeeper willing to help with the Malian bees. A leading light in one of the Casamance Beekeepers' Co-operative was a man called Ousmane Sembene. He was very experienced and also of mixed Manding and Peuhl ethnic stock. This meant he was remotely related to the people in Mali and spoke their language along with several other dialects.

When I asked him to go and share his experience, he was agreeable but slightly concerned about who would look after his own hives in his absence. The mention of a small salary decided the matter. If he could afford to pay someone to keep an eye on things while he was away, he was definitely willing to go. I had no doubt he would employ a minor relation, but had no objection to this. That he was willing to go was what mattered.

I FLEW ON TO DAKAR FOR meetings with the government about the next phase of the Senegal River clean water project, and returned four days later to pick up Ousmane. He had never been in an aeroplane, but seemed totally relaxed as we flew west into Mali. It was interesting hearing his observations on how the countryside and the vegetation changed as we reached the headwaters of the River Niger. His perspective made me look at the landscape with new eyes. There's no limit, I realised, to whom one can learn from, and this man taught me a lot.

I wondered how he would get on with the sorcerer, as Ousmane was a steadfast mission-educated Catholic.

We weren't going anywhere near airports and officials on this trip and I hoped nobody would make waves about my bringing Ousmane across the frontier with no papers. The village of Kengebu was isolated and had never seen a policeman, so I expected nobody would even know, let alone mind.

I'd dropped off the beehives on my way to Senegal; they were all stored in Akleno's compound. He had agreed to wait until I brought Ousmane before taking them to the orchards. He welcomed us warmly and was delighted to discover he and Ousmane could converse easily. This cut me out of some discussions but there was no point in delegating and then trying to hang onto control.

The bonds between the two grew even stronger that evening when Akleno brought out his kora. Ousmane immediately said that if he had known he would have brought his own instrument. Passing the kora back and forth, the two treated us to a virtuoso recital.

I saw Etu hovering in the shadows, uncertain what to make of this outsider. He had been as reserved with me at the beginning, but gradually softened and then opened up when he saw the initiation brand on my shoulder. Maybe this music would make him friendly towards the man from Casamance. That was only four hundred miles away, after all.

He was there the next morning, skulking at the rear of a long file of villagers trooping off toward the orange groves, each with a beehive on their head. I ran and caught up with him and we had a long talk all the way to the first grove. He had learned that Ousmane was a Catholic and this obviously made him wary. He looked doubtful even when I explained that although this was so, there were many sorcerers in his part of Senegal and his faith wouldn't stop him respecting what others believed. Catholics understand spirits; they had a whole host of saints themselves.

However hard I tried to convince him, Etu maintained his doubt. I told him I would call him Thomas as long as he persisted, and told him the story of doubting Thomas. He smiled and said this was like the story of Oku'un, who was left behind at the beginning of the world when the spirits were given their natures. When Oku'un came to ask for his, all the other natures had been taken and there seemed to be nothing left. So he became the spirit of empty space. He was unable to believe this was a real nature until the gods took him and flew round the world to show him that there was more empty space than places that were filled, with the world being so new. Only then did Oku'un believe. After that he went out and occupied all the empty space and became one of the biggest and best known spirits as a result.

Akleno must have said something to Ousmane about the orange groves having once had a curse on them because when they reached the first trees, he set aside a number of hives and looked round for the sorcerer. When Etu came up, he asked him to seek permission from the spirits to place the hives among the trees. Etu was suspicious. I looked at him sternly and said "Thomas!" Then he got into his stride and gave a great performance. Whatever he did had some effect as I could feel the air crackling and sense movement among the branches. Something was darting about too fast to see but always in the periphery of vision. Something was very excited. It could only be the spirits.

His ritual finished, Etu told Ousmane to place his hand against each tree where he wanted to put a hive and wait until his fingers tingled. Then he could place the hive in the branches. These trees were alive with symbiotic fire ants and I wondered whether it would be ants biting or spirits granting permission that Ousmane would feel first. There was no point in speculating; it was better to do as Etu had said and leave some things to the realm of mystery.

Ousmane went through the grove choosing trees at well-spaced intervals. He didn't get bitten by the fire ants, but then neither did he actually place any of the hives; he got the villager who was carrying each one to put it in the tree, explaining the hive's positioning and care as he went.

When we got back to the village, Ousmane showed them how to use smoke to make the bees placid. In this way, each villager became responsible for looking after one hive and the whole enterprise became a community co-operative. Ousmane was not the leader of his co-operative in Senegal for nothing. Its ethos had become part of his soul. Catholicism, it seemed, had limits.

I STAYED FOR TWO DAYS and then, leaving Ousmane in the village, flew back to Anéhigouya to retrieve my Land Rover and drive to northern Ghana to visit a project there. On my way back from Ghana, I called at Bobo-Dioulasso, collected the honey centrifuge and the wax mangle, together with a few smoke pots and other pieces of incidental equipment and headed back to the village by road. This time Albert came with me. His wife had gone back to Hungary to attend to family business, and he was on his own. He was due some leave as he had not taken any for over two years, and he fancied a bush trip.

Albert had made another machine for extracting orange oil and had also built a small hand-cranked centrifuge to enable the oil to be spin-cleaned. Now he was keen to see them in use.

The atmosphere was slightly subdued when we reached the village. Nasia was waiting, her face sombre and her clothes looking torn. The news was not good: Ayenu was dead. He had been bitten by a snake five days earlier. Realising his time had come, he had set out to walk to the stick hut, so that he could pass easily through the gateway and become an ancestor. He had fallen on the way, broken his leg and died in the open bush. He was found later that day by one of the village children who ran to the village with the news.

Nasia's distress was not because he had died – she knew his time had come – but for the manner of his death. There had been no time to prepare him and Inyati had not been warned. Without his guidance, Ayenu's spirit was at risk and his transition to the ancestors could have been traumatic. He deserved better than that.

She told me the man from Senegal – Nasia always referred to Ousmane like this – had been kind. He collected Ayenu's body, took him to the stick hut and said prayers over him. She missed her oldest companion, feeling frail and vulnerable without him. I wrapped my arms around her and held her for a long while, sharing a little of her grief while Albert unloaded the equipment from the Land Rover.

Ousmane's news was better. Several of the new hives had been occupied by wild swarms and the bees were busy constructing neat honeycombs on the frames inside. He had high hopes that within three months there would be a good supply of honey in these hives. He was already planning more hives in the other orchards and wanted a supply of materials so they could be made here in the village. This was slightly problematic as we were a long way from the nearest road, let alone a town where it might be possible to buy boards. I promised to look into the matter.

Ousmane also wanted jars for the honey. The youngsters had located some huge wild hives which probably contained many kilos of honey. He intended to find their queens and transfer them and their swarms into new hives. The honeycombs would provide a valuable source of beeswax and fresh honey. By slicing the wild combs into flat segments, he thought it should be possible to use the frame centrifuge to extract the honey. He also planned to roll blocks of beeswax we had brought with the mangle and teach the villagers how to load wax starter sheets into the frames.

The honey project was going well. For this community to prosper, all we needed was a positive response from Marcel Dupuy in Paris.

Albert and I spent two days in the village before returning to Bobo-Dioulasso. On the way, we stopped in Ouelessebougou and bought some plywood sheets, making arrangements for these to be cut into specific-sized pieces: kits for Ousmane's new hives.

PASSING THROUGH OUAHIGOUYA on my way home, I called at the PTT and found a long telex from Marcel, half of which was *parfumiers'* gobbledygook and made no sense to me. There was one section, however, that made lots of sense and pleased me enormously: the offer to buy ten litres of orange oil a year at a price of 2,550 francs per litre, to be sent to Paris in five two-litre lots. The offer required oil of a consistent standard and only from the blue and the yellow labelled trees, in equal quantities. He also wanted ten kilos of honey with each delivery of oil.

The telex included a lot of verbiage about how the oil should be packaged and shipped, but these were administrative details I could attend to later. Further down he asked me to try drying some of the orange blossom to see if that could also make a viable source of fragrance and he went into some detail about how to do this. This part, he explained, was purely experimental. He would pay shipping costs for any blossom we dried, but would not pay for the work involved in drying it.

This was wonderful news. I wished there was a means of sending word rapidly to Akleno and the villagers, but that would have to wait. Work in Ghana and Niger needed my attention and would keep me occupied for the next month. After that, I would fly down to take Ousmane home to Senegal. The good news would have to keep until then.

29 ~ The price of success

MY PLANE WAS IDEAL FOR landing on unprepared strips so I managed to land on a rather lumpy road just outside Ouelessebougou without too much difficulty. The plywood had been cut and was ready for collection. I managed to load half of it into the plane and fly on to the village with it. Flying back to the town to collect the rest, I took Ousmane with me so that he could get some incidental supplies like nails, wire and other small items he needed.

He had done a good job teaching the villagers about beekeeping and had organised their activities so the responsibility was widely shared. Every family in the village now had an interest in the project. So far they had found five wild colonies with large full honeycombs. Ousmane had taught them how to find the queen and move her to a new hive so that the rest of the swarm would follow. They had managed successfully to transfer four swarms to new hives. He was trying to select young grubs that could grow into new queens to populate hives of their own, but this had not yet been successful. On his next visit he would bring some from Senegal.

Ousmane had agreed to return in three months to see how things were progressing. In the meantime, I was to find a way of commercialising the venture so that excess honey could be sold and generate a proper cash economy for the village, in the same way it had for the Casamance Beekeepers' Co-operative in Senegal. Ousmane was pleased the French had decided to buy the orange oil, though he didn't have much faith in that as a commercial venture. He was much more interested in the honey because he understood bees and honey, and knew there was a viable product there.

That evening, I asked the headman to call the villagers together, to tell them about Marcel Dupuy's offer and to discuss the future. The honey project had become popular because every family was involved. Besides what the French were going to buy, there would to be some honey left over for eating, and everyone loved honey.

The money the orange oil would bring was welcome, but I sensed a slight reserve. The machine was fiddly to operate, it needed constant cleaning and the amount of oil produced from each orange was very small. It meant a lot of fruit had to be picked and processed to get any return. On top of that, since Marcel had colour-coded the trees and only wanted the oil from about a third of them, it left many trees unexploited. For people who had previously ignored these trees so completely, I found it curious that they should now feel so sensitive about only partial exploitation. Maybe greed was a fundamental emotion.

The villagers expressed a little more interest when I explained about collecting and drying the flowers, but after some discussion they decided it was an activity for the children. They could collect the flowers and dry them, but only from the trees that were not being used for oil; otherwise the trees would not produce enough oranges to produce the oil.

It was when I went to wash myself later that an old idea came back to me. I was using a bar of soap I had brought from Dogbo-Itémé and the scent of orange reminded me there could be other uses for the oil. If the villagers were willing to extract oil from the fruit of the other coloured trees, it might be possible to sell this to the women in Dahomey for their soap. It wouldn't make as much money as the French were offering for the premium product, but it would bring in a cash income and support a good rural industry.

I took a small bottle of orange oil to show the soap ladies when I next visited Dogbo-Itémé to find out how the laundry was progressing.

30 ~ Dénouement

THE FRENCH FRAGRANCE house Parfums Fragigny bought orange oil from the villagers for three years. In 1976, Lucien Dréfault, who was senior partner in the business and somewhat older than Marcel Dupuy, had a stroke. While he recovered well, it left him with less energy and enthusiasm for work so he decided to retire, moving back to his family home near Nancy in the east of France. Marcel Dupuy struggled on alone for a while but, despite his wonderful nose for perfumes, he was not an astute businessman like his former partner. The enterprise declined and he sold the business to one of the bigger perfume makers. Marcel continued working for the new owners, but after six months, he decided he didn't fit and retired to the penthouse of the ten-storey apartment block he owned. There he was able to live off the rent paid by his tenants and grow beautifully scented roses on his roof garden.

The new owners of the perfume business weren't interested in wild orange oil; it didn't fit their fragrance profile. They preferred more commercial sources and already used similar products from estates in Spain. They stopped buying from Mali and even argued over paying for the last shipment.

It happened that I had to make a trip to London while that was going on, so I diverted through Paris and sat on the new chairman's desk until he agreed to pay up. He tried to fob me off with a promise and a letter, but I insisted. After a three-hour stand-off, he called his accountant, telling him to bring a pile of nice crisp ten franc notes to his office. This worthy counted out four hundred and seventy of these banknotes to cover the cost of two litres of oil plus the shipping charges. Before I left, I also made him sign a letter transferring ownership of the processing machines in perpetuity to the villagers.

They never found another market among the *parfumiers* of Paris, but the villagers continued to produce small quantities of orange oil which they sold to soap-makers across West Africa. The largest of these customers was in Dahomey.

Etu was disappointed when the French withdrew. He swore to put a curse on any Frenchman who might come looking for products from their orange groves in the future. It amused me when he called the trees 'their' orange groves. Apparently once the enchantment had been lifted, ownership had become important.

Nasia lived past ninety and died, as she had predicted, peacefully in her sleep a week before her great-granddaughter gave birth. The new baby, her seventh great-great-grandchild, was named Nasia.

Glossary

affal – an alcoholic brew made from forest fruits and bark by the women of Dogbo-Itémé.

balafon – a percussion instrument like a xylophone with gourds hanging below the keys to provide soft resonance.

griots – traditional musicians and story tellers.

kora – the Mandinka harp. Comprising half a large dried gourd, covered with hide and with a long neck fitted, it has two rows of six strings each over a high bridge. The gourd is rested against the musician's belly and the instrument it played with the thumbs.

nsu – aromatic leaves that produce insect repellent smoke.

parfumiers – blenders of aromatic substances to make perfume.

puirt a beul – mouth music (Gaellic) – pronounced 'poosht-a-bail'.

shinga'a – glossy leaves growing commonly on small plants in the bush. Used by some tribes as an aromatic cooking wrap and in several traditional medicines.

sokago – the wandering sickness.

strigil – a flat blade used by the Romans to clean their skin by scraping when bathing. Working like a small windscreen wiper, it was a useful way of scraping oil from the inside surfaces of the collecting machine's cover.

tokoli – a bad spirit that hangs around after death because it can find no rest, having failed to be accepted by the ancestors or because it died under unnatural circumstances (usually human intervention).

Acknowledgements

MOST OF THOSE WHO SHOULD be thanked for this book are no longer with us, for they are the people and sorcerers among whom the events described took place. Their contribution and the warm welcome they extended to me, by allowing me to participate in their lives, is nevertheless worthy of acknowledgement and lasting gratitude.

Although he too is among the departed, I would nevertheless like to express my thanks to George Cansdale for teaching me about sub-sand abstraction filtration and for helping me make this a viable process in the African bush. His enthusiasm and encouragement were unfailing and the knowledge of snakes he shared saved my life on more than one occasion.

Etienne Mogo, a friend of many years and a native of Lokossa, made available his detailed knowledge of the Dahomeyan spirit world to check my facts and guide my descriptions, ensuring that I have accurately portrayed the people of Dogo-Itémé and their customs. My thanks also to Tim Butcher for allowing me to use his photos of the devil.

Others have helped too, by reading my text, pointing out when it was difficult to follow and helping me correct the ever-present typographic errors. Among them is Helen Hicks, the first person to read the full manuscript, whose comments were particularly helpful. Thanks also to my regular readers, Jenny and Alan Brand, for straining their eyes with intensive copy reading and for their helpful comments.

Thanks also to my many writing friends around the world for their tremendous encouragement and enthusiasm for my writing, especially Sharon Lippincott, whose constructive comments and encouragement, together with her treatise on descriptive writing, helped me think in a new light about what I am writing and thereby develop my style.

A book like this could not exist without the infinite patience of others, particularly my editor and publisher, Chuck Grieve, who makes working with him a pleasure rather than a burden. While the regular consumption of fine coffee and wide-ranging chats over many topics has always helped lubricate this relationship, a never-ending stream of e-mails has enabled us to sort out points of detail with ease, and his skill and dedication as an editor have lifted my manuscripts from a scrawl to become the books of this African Memoir series.

Lastly, I must thank my lovely wife, Gay, without whose untiring and continual love and support none of my books would ever have been written, let alone seen print.

Lightning Source UK Ltd.
Milton Keynes UK
UKOW04f0254130314

228019UK00001B/6/P